SHAH JAHAN

SHAH JAHAN

A PLAY IN FIVE ACTS

BY

L. STANLEY JAST

Formerly Chief Librarian of Manchester,
Past President of the Library Association

Author of
"Libraries and Living,"
"The Lover and the Dead Woman," etc.

GYAN

Published by

Gyan Publishing House
5, Ansari Road
Daryaganj, New Delhi-110002
Phone: 011-47034999, 9811692060
E-mail: books@gyanbooks.com

Distribution Network
gyanbooks.com
India, USA, Canada, UK, Australia, France

ISBN : 978-81-212-2584-7 (HB)
First Published, 1934

2nd Impression 2021

Printed at: Gyan Press, Delhi.

Shah Jahan
Author: L. Stanley Jast

SHAH JAHAN

A PLAY IN FIVE ACTS

by

L. STANLEY JAST

Formerly Chief Librarian of Manchester,
Past President of the Library Association

Author of
"Libraries and Living,"
"The Lover and the Dead Woman," etc.

LONDON
GRAFTON & CO.
51, GREAT RUSSELL STREET
1934

This play was produced by the Unnamed Society, at their Little Theatre, Manchester, on January 14th, 1929.

To

MY WIFE

MILLICENT JAST (*née* MURBY)

If aught in this is worthy thee,
'Tis thine! The rest remains to me.

PREFACE

In a notice of the performance of this play by the Unnamed Society, in Manchester, the critic of a dramatic weekly referred to it as a "chronicle play." This is exactly what *Shah Jahan* is not. A chronicle play takes certain scenes from history, with in general an adherence to the facts, so far as these are assumed to be known. There is in consequence no plot, and the action merely happens. It just was so. It is only in rare cases that history apes the imaginative artist, and constructs as carefully as he. Shakespeare's *Henry VIII* is a chronicle play, so is Drinkwater's *Cromwell*, or *Abraham Lincoln*. In *Shah Jahan* I have taken history as merely supplying the raw material of my play, and I have not hesitated to shape that material exactly as I pleased to suit the purposes of the action. If in doing this I have achieved an approximate truth of atmosphere and of character (the latter as I have conceived it) I have done all I intended to do, and as much I maintain as any "chronicle play" ever does. Nothing can be more misleading than "the truth of facts," seeing that (1) the facts are never accurately known, and (2) whatever significance they may have is due to the temperamental content imparted by the historian or the artist.

It is unnecessary to mention in detail where and how I have departed from the historic record which has come down to us. The reader acquainted with the confused and blood-stained annals of the Mogul emperors will not require it, and the reader not so acquainted won't care. Two points, however, I will notice. The Christian motive in the play I have transplanted from the reign of Akbar, where it was a real political issue. Jahan may be assumed to have inherited

Akbar's delight in staging religious discussions. That Mumtaz Mahal, "the Lady of the Taj," should have died within a little more than three years of Jahan's occupancy of the throne, is one of the unfortunate blunders of the historic muse. But it seemed to me that a play about one of the most magnificent builders and lovers that the world has seen *without* the lady who inspired him would be artistically untrue. She lived undoubtedly for Jahan, and she therefore lives in the play. Nor would her death while accompanying Jahan on one of his military expeditions (which was actually the case) have had any dramatic significance. This too then I have ordered otherwise. For the rest, there are few incidents in the play for which history has not supplied some sort of basis or suggestion.

The play was written for the stage, unlikely as it is in days when the poetic play has fallen on evil times, that it should attain production in a more public theatre than that which saw its original performance. My debt to the Unnamed Society for its courage in putting it on, and for the success which attended it, is the greater.

L. S. J.

BECKINGTON,
BATH.

CHARACTERS OF THE PLAY

SHAH JAHAN, *Emperor of Hindostan*

DARA
AURUNGZEB } *Sons of Shah Jahan*

JAFAR KHAN, *Prime Minister*

BAHLOL, *A Eunuch*

FATHER BUSEO, *a Jesuit Priest*

THE MULLAH

A YOGI

MIR JUMLA, *a General*

AN OFFICER OF DARA'S

AN OFFICER OF AURUNGZEB'S

A SOLDIER

A PAGE

MESSENGER

MUMTAZ MAHAL, *Empress of Hindostan*

HIRA BAI
AKBARABADI
FATHPURI } *Wives of Shah Jahan*

JAHANARA, *Daughter of Shah Jahan*

ACT I

Scene i

AGRA. *An apartment in the zenana. It is partly open to the sky, and a small fountain plays in the centre.*

AKBARABADI, HIRA BAI, FATHPURI, *afterwards* BAHLOL, SHAH JAHAN.

AKBARABADI (*to* HIRA BAI) : Do you beware,
Lest the red blood of passion end in blood.
HIRA BAI : Whose ?
AKBARABADI : Yours.
HIRA BAI : Not a whit.
I shall die kissing, or I'll lie me down,
Weary with loving, and so faint to death.
AKBARABADI : The prince will out of question stop that gap
Even as 'tis made.
HIRA BAI : But not with you, not
With any of you.
AKBARABADI : And yet
He has looked on me with a most meaning eye.
HIRA BAI : You mean you have looked on him,
And your hot ardour shining on his face,
Reflected back from that unconscious glass,
Has made your fire seem his.
AKBARABADI : No woman looks on woman with that eye.
HIRA BAI (*approaching her menacingly*) : You . . .
(AKBARABADI *shrinks away.*)
Sick lust,
Feeding itself on dreams.

FATHPURI : The faithfullest men are faithless with their eyes.

HIRA BAI : But not the emperor.
We are but day wives to the emperor.
He is not even negligently fond,
But concentrates his love and manliness
On the queen,
As she were his harem, and we
Her maids and dressers.

FATHPURI : Nor concubines nor wives are we,
But virgins wedded.

HIRA BAI : Fools, why then keep what is your shame to keep?
We are only husband-bound, not husbanded,
And he, our lord, tastes not of our sweet fruit,
But sucks the harvest of one single tree,
And will not glance away.
Must then the orchard rot,
And the worms canker us, ere our young blood
Has rushed the heart of love?
Ye are not women, but pale ghosts are ye,
And thinly live on unsubstantial air.
Why have ye women's motions, women's breasts,
And rosy limbs, and wine-empurpled lips,
Is it enough to feed some wandering eye?
Were not we made for men, and men for us,
And if our stream is dammed, shall we not turn
The rock that bars our flow?

FATHPURI : If it were but a little snag, why, yes;
But 'tis the earth which lords us, and on him
We hang like water-drops.

HIRA BAI : We are his ribbons which he wears for show.

FATHPURI : Wears while unspotted, but if soiled
He tears us.

AKBARABADI (*to* HIRA BAI) : As he will you,
If that your amour with Prince Aurungzeb
Comes to his ears.

HIRA BAI : You jade,
    Hiss you that out so loudly.
    I'll tell the prince, and have you,
    For scandalling him and his most mighty father,
    Buried to the neck in sand,
    The hot sun shining on your naked head,
    Till it is one huge blister ;
    And so in dumb and airless agony
    Shall you turn black and perish.
AKBARABADI (*weeping*) : Oh ! Oh ! Oh !
FATHPURI : You've frightened her. You should not
    Speak her so roughly.
HIRA BAI : The puling wretch. I would not be
    Such watery stuff as she is made on
    For Jahan's treasure vault.
AKBARABADI : Oh ! Oh ! Oh !
HIRA BAI : Mop up your passion, or your cries
    Will bring Bahlol.

[*Enter* BAHLOL.]

BAHLOL : What's this ? What's this ?
    You quarrelling cats. I'll have the emperor
    To curb you, for as Allah knows
    The wits of this poor eunuch cannot do it.
FATHPURI : If Allah knows, the emperor
    Knows not, nor cares whether we weep or smile.
BAHLOL : Why should he, for what women do
    Concerns the devil only. Do or do not,
    It is his work that's done.
HIRA BAI : A eunuch's fit for nothing save to talk.
BAHLOL : Ha ! you voluptuous minions, have a care
    Your acts are virtuous as your thoughts are not.
    The emperor's here anon. You'd better go,
    Seeing that he hates the sight of you.
    No wonder either.

HIRA BAI : Your hate is longing, his
Is Mumtaz' witch-craft, which befogs his eye,
And clouds his manhood that he heeds us not.
We are as fair as she.
FATHPURI : The air is cold already. Let us hence
Ere that he freezes us.
HIRA BAI : I will stand my ground.
FATHPURI : He will not look on you, or if he does
'Twill be as if he gazed upon a stool,
Or anything that has no sentience in it.
HIRA BAI : He shall not. I'm a woman, and I have
The graces of a woman, and I'll draw
His eyes upon my beauties—and who knows,
His senses may forget themselves and be
My momentary subjects.
BAHLOL : Ha ! Ha ! Ha ! Jahan
Will king your insolence, or I'm a man
And not a eunuch. But I had forgot.
(*to* HIRA BAI)
I have a writing for you Aurungzeb
Bade me deliver. (*Giving her a letter*). That's a game
Wherein the odds are death.
HIRA BAI : Silence, ugly slave,
Or Aurungzeb shall learn you have a tongue
That wags too much.
BAHLOL (*cringing*) : Suspect me not. I am
Devoted both to Aurungzeb and you.
HIRA BAI : 'Tis well for you he thinks so. (*Noise of steps off.*)
BAHLOL : Here's the king.
[AKBARABADI *and* FATHPURI *hurriedly go off. Enter* SHAH JAHAN.]
HIRA BAI : I kiss your majesty's feet. We have been dull
Without our lord and master.
JAHAN : Where are the other women ?
HIRA BAI : They fled your majesty's presence, like the stars
When the sun rises.

JAHAN : One star yet shines it seems.

HIRA BAI : So dazzled, majesty, its winking light
Tell-tales its heart's confusion.

[*She poses alluringly.* JAHAN *regards her with complete indifference.*]

JAHAN : It is no matter. Where is the empress ?

HIRA BAI : In the Jasmine Tower, majesty.

JAHAN (*murmuring to himself*) : Beauty in beauty's shrine.
I who built it for her never
Packed so much loveliness in stone as when
I thought of Mumtaz, and the thought became
A wonder-bower. I will seek her there.

[*Exit* JAHAN.]

BAHLOL : Ha ! Ha ! Ha ! Ha !
Better to be a eunuch,
Than be a woman with her wares despised,
Than be a wife whose husband sees her not.

HIRA BAI : Dost laugh, you ape ?
Laughter becomes not slaves.
If they break silence, it should be with howls.
You shall make proper music.

[*She beats him, and he howls lustily as the scene closes.*]

SCENE 2

AGRA. *An apartment in the Empress's quarters—known as the Jasmine Tower.*

SHAH JAHAN, MUMTAZ MAHAL, PAGE.

JAHAN : It is a false dawn till I greet my love,
For then begins the day.

MUMTAZ : So may it ever be with thee and me,
And when it is not,
Let my life follow my love,
And one stone cover both.

JAHAN : Fear not.
If we're immortal, so's our love,
And if love die,
It perishes with the source of it, our hearts.

MUMTAZ : Do you believe, Jahan,
That love like ours can perish ?
Say you do not.
For e'en the thinking that a thing so fair
Hath fellowship in corruption with our flesh
Is as a kind of taint, a treason,
Hidden in the very core of it, which doth unquality
Its strain and lustre.

JAHAN : Is love not all-sufficient to itself
Because it is ? The past and future,
The twin begetters of all hopes and fears,
Take from the perfect momentary now,
Which if love fills with its o'erbrimming measure
The thought of surcease cannot enter there,
And we are timeless like eternity.
So—are you answered ?

MUMTAZ : It is my heart which questioned, and to that
You have not spoken.
A woman's love, Jahan,
Is made of hopes and fears. There's nothing
That touches him she loves or moves him but,
Like air upon a flame, its faintest breath
Is followed by a leaping sympathy.
To tell me then I must not fear nor hope,
Is to tell me not to love.

JAHAN : Which were to say unto the nightingale,
Sing not ; to tell the moon
To empty all her beams of mystery ;
Command the soft gazelle to be ungentle ;
And every natural thing to rend his nature
And be not what it is.

MUMTAZ : The nightingale
Hath but one listener to his amorous song,
And in the whole of Heaven there's but one moon.
Ah, happy nightingale, ah, happy moon.
JAHAN : What matter that a man has many wives,
So that one woman is the absolute she,
The others,
Mere shapes to his indifferent eye,
When seen unnoticed, and when heard unmarked.
MUMTAZ : And yet—
Oh see, Jahan, how love makes women fearful—
How oft a shape passed by a thousand times
Takes substance suddenly, springing
Out of the darkness of indifference
Into a high relief,
And that which was the knot and goal of vision
Holds its proud place no more.
Jahan has younger, fairer wives
Than this Mumtaz ; he like the moon
Shines down on many brooks, the brook
Sees but one moon.
JAHAN : What—what—to so misjudge
Jahan and Jahan's race!
My dynasty is famed for constancy.
Was not my father, Jahangir,
Notorious faithful to a single face,
My mother—Nour Mahal.
If I am warrior, ruler, conqueror,
It is because I must ; bloody and cruel
Because my subjects are so, for they make
Their kings in their own likeness—faugh!
Beasts must be ruled by beasts.
We mount and ride them
Lest they should tear their masters.
But myself,
Jahan's Jahan,

I laugh at conquerors,
Who heap up earth to strut on it and die.
I am an artist, and I worship beauty,
Worship it, and create it.
The real Jahan is in my palaces,
And in my love of thee.
I write my name—the name of Shah Jahan—
In the enduring fabric of my marbles,
And when the empire of our Mogul line
Crumbles in the inevitable flux of time,
And Akbar and Jahangir are but words
That monarchise in musty chronicles,
Men still shall say,
Jahan built this, and this,
These dreams in stone were dreamed by Shah Jahan,
Jahan of one unalterable love, the which
He treasured more than these ;
The greatest builder and the greatest lover
That ever walked the earth. Thy boy
Shall lute and sing to thee the scented script
Wherein my love is writ. What, boy !

MUMTAZ : Emperor of words !

JAHAN : Not so ; commanded words are cold,
But unto lovers they yield up themselves,
Distilling willingly their fragrances.
All lovers must be poets, for all love
Is poetry in action. None so poor,
But whiles they love are lifted from themselves.
Beggars are kings, and kings,
Deeming their kingships beggarly, are Gods.
There is a star on every lover's brow,
That gives even to unnoticeable men
Something to mark them by, and mouths all dumb
Conceive the trick of music.
Sing boy !

[*The* PAGE *sings to the accompaniment of the lute.*]

SONG.

Love is as old as man,
But since this love began
None loved like Shah Jahan,
Like Shah Jahan.

Soft are the eyes that gleam
In Shah Jahan's harem.
They pass as in a dream
By Shah Jahan.

One only fair he knows,
One only flower that blows,
The world has but one rose
For Shah Jahan.

None other can contest
The kingdom of his breast,
Of all the loveliest,
Mumtaz Mahal.

Love is as old as man,
But since the world began
None loved like Shah Jahan,
Like Shah Jahan.

[*With the ending of the song the scene closes,* JAHAN *embracing* MUMTAZ *passionately during the last verse.*]

Scene 3

Agra. *The Hall of Private Audience. A balcony is indicated on the left. One or two small tables, on one of which is wine. When the scene opens* Jahan *is pacing the chamber, musing.* Bahlol *stands at the rear.*

Shah Jahan, Bahlol, *afterwards* Jafar Khan, Aurungzeb, Father Buseo, Hira Bai.

Jahan : When majesty is seated on his throne
The throne becomes an accident, a property,
That subserves majesty, like to his robes,
His crown, or anything that's his,
Trifles that do take their all of awe
From him they hang on. But when
The throne is empty of its living state,
It then becomes majesty's substitute,
The very altar of his sovereignty,
The sign and sum of loftiness and power.
'Tis fitting then that the inheritor
Of Akbar and Jahangir, in whose time and person
Empire has risen upon empire,
And glory's footstool is itself a glory,
Should have his visible emblem in a throne
That shall out-stare all other thrones soever,
And level them to ordinary seats
For ordinary kings. I'll fashion one
I' the semblance of a peacock,
And outbid nature's colours with her jewels.
The throne, the peacock throne of Shah Jahan :
I'll bid my jeweller design it straight,
And think in diamonds, rubies, pearls,
Sapphires, and topazes, and emeralds,
Till his imagination can no more.
Already am I blinded by the thought of it,
And wink as it were there.

[*Enter* JAFAR KHAN.]

JAFAR : I greet your majesty.

JAHAN (*still absorbed*) : The throne, the peacock throne of
Shah Jahan.

JAFAR : The King
Designs some new magnificence. Have not we yet
Reached to the top of wonder ?

JAHAN : No. No. No.
Wonder has but a momentary life,
And quickly perishes if it be not fed
With still more wonders. But you've news, my friend ;
To stab my ears or tickle them ?

JAFAR : Both.

JAHAN : Then stab them first. Pleasure's more pleasurable
When it's the follower not the lead of pain.

JAFAR : The prince Dara
Has once more bit the dust at Kandahar.
The Persians hold it stronglier than ever,
And our troops waste away. The prince
Says 'tis impregnable and desires return.

JAHAN : He is a bungler,
Better as a philosopher than a soldier.
I must and will have Kandahar again.
'Twas Akbar's trophy, and my father lost it.
It shames me
To spend such blood and treasure for a gesture,
That they may laugh in Persia.
I will send Aurungzeb
And Kandahar shall mark his soldiership.

JAFAR : Is it wise
To set the younger o'er the elder brother ?

JAHAN : That's a nice point we can't consider now.
If Aurungzeb does capture Kandahar
He'll be the elder in accomplishment.
We'll act at once.

(*To* Bahlol)
Summon the prince to me.
[*Exit* Bahlol.]
What is your other news ?
Jafar : The priest from Goa
Has come, and waits on you.
Jahan : The good father
Shall have informal audience presently.
Jafar : The *good* father ?
He's good if we do find him good.
I do distrust these Portugals.
They creep upon us, they and the English,
Spreading like a disease from spot to spot.
These animals from the sea are dangerous,
Waxing more insolent as they do grow
In number and in ships.
Jahan : Fear not the father. He's a man of God.
Jafar : We have too many men of God already,
Of godly men too few. Is't not enough
To have Hindu, Parsee, Mohammedan,
And various nondescript rag-tails of holiness,
That we must learn from these barbarians
Another way to pray ?
Jahan : Pleases the queen, my friend, pleases the queen.
Jafar : But pleases not your subjects, majesty,
For whiles they fervently damn one another,
They'll all unite in damning this same priest,
And that's not politic.
Jahan : Not politic ? What am I then,
A subject with a crown on, or a king,
Who'll make that politic which pleases him.
You offer craven counsel. Lock it up
And fling away the key.
Bahlol (*re-entering*) : Prince Aurungzeb.
[*Enter* Aurungzeb.]

JAHAN : Aurungzeb,
You rust in court. Your brother Dara
Scratches against the walls of Kandahar
And hurts himself and us.
Take you command, and with a thrustier sword,
Pick up the city on the point of it.

AURUNGZEB : Your majesty,
When Dara fails, shall Aurungzeb succeed ?
Leave me to tell my beads, to fast and pray.
When I am holier, then I'll fight for you,
For God will be my arm. Had Dara
Followed the one true God with piety,
He would have crushed the Persian infidels.

JAHAN : Your head and will, and what I will provide you
In men and the fell instruments of war,
Shall serve our purpose, and your trust in God
Your own. Be ready to set out.

AURUNGZEB : Alas ! how difficult it is for princes
To lose the world and all its vanities.
And Dara ?

JAHAN : Serves under you, or if
His temper more imperious than his deeds
Brooks not your over-lording, let him home,
To hide him with his women.

AURUNGZEB : Poor, poor Dara.

JAHAN : When next I hear the name of Kandahar,
Let it sound proudly.
(*To* BAHLOL)
Bring the father in.

AURUNGZEB : May God confound all infidels,
All heretics and schisms.

[*Enter* BAHLOL *and* FATHER BUSEO.]

BAHLOL : Father Buseo.

JAHAN : You are welcome to my court.

BUSEO : From the archbishop of Goa
I bring you loving greetings,

And your request to send to you a priest,
It is God's call, and I
Am the most humble and unworthy answer.

JAHAN : The more unworthy in your own esteem,
The worthier in your master's, and in mine.

BUSEO (*handing to* JAHAN *a Bible*) : The archbishop
Begs your august acceptance of this volume,
More precious than the untold wealth which lies
Within the treasure vaults of Shah Jahan,
The holy volume of the Christian faith.

[JAHAN *kisses the Bible, and places it for a moment on his head, in token of reverence. He then lays it on a table.*]

AURUNGZEB (*aside to* JAFAR) : Did you see that ?

JAFAR (*to* AURUNGZEB) : Inform the Mullah that he give Jahan
A Koran finely printed, and mark well
It must be richlier bound.

JAHAN : We thank the archbishop.
My grandfather, the mighty Akbar,
Had at his court some priests of your religion,
Whom he did value highly.

BUSEO : Alas ! great sovereign,
Akbar rejected that they taught to him,
With his own hands did spurn the proffered cup,
Brimmed with the waters of eternal life,
And with his thirsty soul unslaked, unshrived,
Was lost in death.
As you are mightier than preceding kings,
Be mightier in your wisdom.
There is but one true faith, O King,
The faith of Jesus,
Whereto it is my fervent, blessed task
To lead you, lord, if that your noble heart
Shall open to your Saviour's gentle touch,
And so by your example,
Your country too.

AURUNGZEB : Never ! insolent priest,
Akbar who banished you
Had learned his wisdom then.
JAHAN : Content you, Aurungzeb,
You are too hasty and too positive.
As for me, good father,
I am much bewildered.
There are so many Gods, so many Saviours,
So many faiths, so many one true ways,
But which is *the* way is a knotty point.
We'll have you, if it is your pleasure,
As it is ours, argue with t'other priests
And holy men,
Who's right, who's wrong, as to the which
Our mind is like a vexed and puzzled traveller,
Waiting his certain road. Meantime,
The queen's desire to see and talk with you
Must be no more extended.
Myself will take you. Aurungzeb,
There's a great hole north-west,
Through which our empire leaks,
Plug it with Kandahar.
[*Exit* JAHAN, *followed by* BUSEO *and* JAFAR KHAN.]
AURUNGZEB (*to* BAHLOL) : The Lady Hira Bai,
Has she my message ?
BAHLOL : She has.
AURUNGZEB : The King's will cancels it.
Bid her attend me.
[*Exit* BAHLOL.]
Jahan
Is safely prisoned with his adoration,
And afterwards the public audience
Will hold him fast.
This craze of Jahan's
The queen is privy to.
She much affects the Christians.

Is't idle or of moment? Down,
Gigantic hope; assume
Proportions only of a tiny seed,
And let your substance and my secret hope
Swell comparably.

BAHLOL (*re-entering*): The lady Hira Bai.

[*Enter* HIRA BAI. *Exit* BAHLOL.]

HIRA BAI: Nay, nay, your beck-and-call,
For so you use me, Aurungzeb.
Am I your waiting maid, your dancing girl,
That at your nod I hasten to my master,
And say: here is your chattel,
Do with me as you will, prince Aurungzeb.

AURUNGZEB: I am in haste.

HIRA BAI: Oh! Oh! you are in haste.
And must my leisure wait upon your haste?
Why do you tell me that you are in haste,
When "I must take my leave" is in your look,
Departure written in your very air.
I had a lover once, but he is gone,
Sending a lying message by yon slave,
Whom 'twas my shame to follow.
He should be thrashed
For fooling ladies. (*Going*) I am in haste, haste, haste.

AURUNGZEB: Stay. I do command you stay.

HIRA BAI: Are you the king?
I know you would be king.
Is Shah Jahan cut off,
Dara, and Shuja, Murad, put away?
Why then as I'm the king's wife, I am yours,
And therefore will I be obedient.

AURUNGZEB: You mock me. Not Jahan himself
Is more the subject of Mumtaz
Than Aurungzeb is Hira Bai's.
We are alike in being slaves to women.

HIRA BAI : Women ! Jahan
Knows naught of women.
AURUNGZEB : To one woman, one, one, one woman,
My heart's a ring,
The golden setting of a single stone,
And you that stone. For me
There is no other jewel.
HIRA BAI : The sweet-tongued Aurungzeb.
Fie, fie, you are a saint, an anchorite,
Austere and pious. I would be
The anchorite's temptation.
AURUNGZEB : So you are.
HIRA BAI : 'Twas not a lying message then which came,
And tongue and lips do wait but on the night
To put their deeds to proof ?
AURUNGZEB : A night, yes, yes, but not
This night. I swear I am as much afire as you,
But cold necessity has bid me temper it
Till I have leave to blow it to a flame.
I go immediately to Kandahar.
It is the Emperor's order.
HIRA BAI : Fly to Dara's arms.
To Dara's—not to mine. Since when
Did you love Dara so ?
AURUNGZEB : He is a pestilent heretic, a Sufi,
Worse than a Christian. But I go
To take the high command at Kandahar,
And wash the city clean of Persian filth,
Which Dara has not done and cannot do.
HIRA BAI : And when the conqueror returns ?
AURUNGZEB : 'Tis at your feet he'll lay his soldiership.
HIRA BAI : Would I could wear it to the gaze o' the world !
AURUNGZEB : Art mad ? Then keep your madness
Till it is sane to show it.
HIRA BAI : Fear not for me. Jahan
Has Mumtaz in his eyes. She is

His basilisk,
His wall that shuts him in.

AURUNGZEB: May he dwell always in that citadel.
But do you be my watch.
There's Father Buseo, a Christian priest,
Arrived in Agra, and Jahan
Receives him kindly, nay, has asked for him,
And puts the Christian scriptures on his head,
In token of respect. What comes of that
May touch the kingdom nearly.

HIRA BAI: Say, may touch Aurungzeb, and I must be
Your eye and ear,
Convenient instrument of Aurungzeb's,
A gatherer of chatter and surmise,
And for my payment, in my mouth he pops
A sweetmeat now and then.

AURUNGZEB: What now?

HIRA BAI: Oh, I am richly paid.
He talks of love, says I'm his jewel,
And when my silly, silly little head is turned,
His point discloses, which is policy.
I ask for love, he proffers policy.

AURUNGZEB: How shall I take you? God and His Prophet
Absolve me if I follow you. You have
My sworn and constant love.

HIRA BAI: Words, which as fast as they're expended are reshaped,
And the store loses nothing.

AURUNGZEB: In proper time
I shall fulfil them.

HIRA BAI: Now, now, now.
Fulfil them now, or I'll proclaim you false
Alike in head and heart.

AURUNGZEB: What would you have me do?

HIRA BAI: A little thing, a very little thing.

(*She goes to a table and pours out a cup of wine.*)

Here's wine.
Drink it to me.

AURUNGZEB : Woman,
Would'st have me traitor to my oath ?
God and His Prophet have forbidden it.
'Tis an abomination and a wickedness,
And damns the drinker.

HIRA BAI : All Mussulmen are not as strict as thou.
Do I not sin in listening to your love,
Breaking the seal of my most lawful bond,
That you may put your wax on't ?
Once, once, this once, canst thou not fall with me,
A little, little fall for love of me ?
And after, you shall glut yourself with penance,
And be the saintlier for this single fault,
As is the trick of holier men than thou.
It is not wine you drink, my Aurungzeb,
But my heart's blood, which seeks
To mingle with the lake which is in thine.
Ah, love, I pray you.

AURUNGZEB : Thus then. (*He drinks.*)

HIRA BAI : Now Hira Bai is your Kandahar.
Her walls are down.
She trails the dust before your conquering feet,
At your fell mercy, soldier.

[*She clasps his knees.* AURUNGZEB *in a sudden frenzy of shame and self-reproach flings the cup away and covers his face with his hands.*]

END OF ACT I.

ACT II

SCENE I

AGRA. *The Hall of Private Audience.*

SHAH JAHAN, *the* MULLAH, FATHER BUSEO, JAFAR KHAN, *a* YOGI, BAHLOL.

THE MULLAH (*kneeling before* SHAH JAHAN, *with a Koran in his uplifted hands*) : Lord of the World,
Commander of the Faithful,
Who, like the sky o'ertopping snows of Himalay,
Sees countless kingdoms crouching at your feet,
God and His Prophet,
Who rule, direct, and guide the souls of men,
Have in this holy book,
Inspired by God, and by His Prophet writ,
Made all who read, and reading so believe,
The inheritors of Paradise.
The true believers in your kingdom, majesty,
Pray you to take it, and by your royal mouth
Be the one law declared :
There is no God but God,
And Mahomet is His Prophet.

[JAHAN *takes the Koran.*]

BUSEO : Vile heretic ! You do blaspheme
Thunderously against God,
And give the King
The devil's scripture.

THE MULLAH (*rising*) : Mahomet strike you, infidel !

JAHAN : Peace, peace, ye holy men.
Conviction is a maid that must be wooed,
Not frightened by high words.
We thank you, Mullah,
And place your Koran by the father's Bible.
Observe how quietly they lie together.

MULLAH (*aside to* JAFAR KHAN) : He has not placed the Koran on his head
As he did place the Bible. Aurungzeb
Told me of that.

JAFAR (*to the* MULLAH) : A straw
Blown by a wind from Goa.
But 'twill change.

JAHAN : All men
Need a religion—kings
No less than beggars, and for us,
Who have most deeply pondered on this theme,
We are like a pendulum, swinging
'Twixt This and That.
So many roads, so many guides,
So many lessons, and so many teachers.
If This is true, That's less than nothing worth ;
If That, then This is cunning false.
How may we from this tempest of opinion
Find the safe shelter ?
Argue, good friends, on that.

YOGI : There is nor This nor That.
Delusions both.
The It alone exists.
'Tis not from scriptures, nor from priests, O King,
You can learn anything.

JAHAN : Why then,
We may not learn from you
That nothing may be learned.
What, Father Buseo ?

BUSEO : It is most fitly answered, majesty,
Whose subjects everywhere contend
Against each other.
High priests and followers of error daily
Wrangle the circling sun.
But in my country there is but one faith,
One God, one Saviour,
Whom all men in one perfect brotherhood
Acclaim and worship.
Is not this then the very seal of truth,
That she has but one voice ?

JAFAR : Are not the English Christians ?
If you love them, is dog a term of love ?
For I have often heard the Portugals
Speak of the English dogs.

BUSEO : The English are not Christians. They are heretics,
And being heretics damned.

YOGI : Heaven and Hell
Are self-created. Fantasies
Wherewith men please and plague their childishness.

BUSEO : Mahomet's paradise indeed is fantasy.
An infamous and carnal house of sin,
Where lights o' love, not wingéd angels, wait
Upon their most lascivious paramours.

MULLAH : Preposterous, upon my beard !
A Heaven without heavenly delights.

BUSEO : A Heaven without lust, and therefore not
Tainted with earthliest pleasures.

MULLAH : Earthliest pleasures ! Do not you Christians,
Nay, even your priests drink wine,
Which makes men mad, muddies the blood
With rank excess, which the Prophet
Commands abstention from.

JAHAN : Blood drawn on both sides, Buseo.
You prick the Mullah with his paradise,
He douses you with wine.

BUSEO : By which I do convict his Prophet, majesty,
Of contradiction flat.
For in th' Koran it is expressly stated
The faithful sup of wine in paradise,
Which it forbids on earth.
JAHAN (*to* THE MULLAH) : What do you say ?
MULLAH : That in this same Koran the Prophet
Speaks of a grapeless wine,
Wherein, O King, it is expressly stated
The faithful are not drunken, nor their minds
Thereby oppressed.
BUSEO : A sea of words, O King, is this Koran,
Which subtle men interpret as they will.
What God inspires can have no double sense,
But all is clear as in our holy book,
Which doth appeal unto the hearts of men, and is not
Cut into them with swords.
MULLAH : Swords ?
BUSEO : Ay. Yours is a bloody faith,
That sabres men till they believe in it.
MULLAH : What ! Wouldst thou not kill God's enemies ?
BUSEO : The meek and gentle Jesus
Said this : Love one another,
And Christians do so.
JAHAN : Is not this a strange wonder, Jafar Khan,
That men love one another over there ?
O lucky kings to rule o'er loving subjects,
And happy subjects to be ruled by love.
'Tis a most excellent religion, Buseo,
And much disposes me.
MULLAH : Majesty,
This cozening priest, whom may the Prophet
Through me confound and silence,
Has in his bosom
A Christian teaching so unnatural-strange,
Opposing reason, virtue, instinct, practice,

That even the vile Hindu would spit on it.
Yea, he would keep it in confinement close,
Till it shall find you in a readier mood,
As poisons given in a growing measure
Make rankest doses prove acceptable.
Hark then ! These Christians do permit
One only wife.

JAFAR : It is impossible.

MULLAH : Most monstrous, nay incredible,
But true.

YOGI : It is a wife too much.
The sage
Abhors all women, for in them
The world's mirage shows fairest.

JAHAN : Answer, Buseo,
How many wives have Christians ?

BUSEO : One, majesty.

JAHAN : Say it again, good father.

BUSEO : One wife, no more.

JAHAN : One wife. A stranger wonder still.

BUSEO : Herein, O King,
Is chaste love from adulterous love divided,
And marriage made a holy sacrament,
Wherein are husband, wife, wife, husband,
Joined in one flesh, one heart,
By God himself, not to be parted
Till death annul the bond.

MULLAH : Monstrous, I say again.

JAFAR : Unnatural.

JAHAN : Say ye so ?
Is not such love the love that I have dreamed,
The love that I have felt and feel ?
A mighty river
That squanders not its waters in the sands,
But empties them into a single breast,
And mingles tide with tide.

JAFAR : But do these Christian husbands
Keep to their bond ?
BUSEO : Do all the followers of Mahomet
Abstain from wine ?
JAHAN : 'Tis a shrewd parry, Jafar, to your thrust.
Now, sirs,
There is a way to clinch your arguments
And satisfy us all.
You, father, with the Bible in your hands,
Which is your talisman ;
(*Giving the Bible to* BUSEO)
You, Mullah, with your Koran guarding you,
(*Giving the Koran to* THE MULLAH)
Shall walk into a fire, which I'll have kindled
Close to our outer gates, whereby the people
Shall see and judge with us.
Who is not burned,
His is the true religion, and I swear,
I, Shah Jahan,
It shall be ours, our court's, our people's.
Consent you, sirs, to this ?
(*A pause*)
Well, well, do you consent to this ?
MULLAH : Let the father
Go in the fire first. If he's not burned,
I will essay the like.
JAHAN : And if he *is* burned, Mullah ?
MULLAH : Why then he's burned for impudently challenging
The Koran and the Prophet.
BUSEO : To serve my Lord, thou minister of lies,
I will most willingly engage the fire,
And die a blesséd martyr for the faith.
JAHAN : Die, Buseo, that is not anything.
Men in this land of India daily die,
Or choose a living torture, serving thus
The God they worship, or but to become

Freed from the limiting body. Thou must live,
Come scatheless through the fire. Thus thou'lt prove
Beyond all question that thy God is God.

BUSEO : It would be impious
To fling such challenge in the face of God.

JAHAN : Why then,
At least ye are agreed, ye holy men,
On this one point, ye will not test the fire.
And so ye burn my hope of harbouring
My wandering ship of doubt to present ashes.
Bahlol, receive the scriptures back again.
For I perceive who would arrive the truth
Must tread the tedious way of words, and faint
Perchance upon the road. Good sirs,
Ye have been valiant warriors of the mouth,
And tongue has clashed with tongue most bloodily.
We call a truce, till leisure and the mood
Again combine. Bid the drums sound,
And we will show ourselves upon the balcony
To all our people. Then
We'll sit i' th' chair of justice and right wrongs,
For so a king must do.

YOGI : A king—a slave.
I am a king, not thou.
Thou art but Shah Jahan,
Whiles I
Am Lord of Nothing, that's the whole, wide world.

[JAHAN *shrugs his shoulders at the* YOGI. *The drums sound loudly as* JAHAN *presents himself on the balcony. Shouts off.* JAHAN *bows and the scene closes.*]

Scene 2

Before Kandahar. *Interior of* Dara's *tent. As the scene opens there is a distant sound of guns mingled with cries.*

Dara, Officer, *afterwards* Aurungzeb.

Dara : How goes the assault,
Advances Aurungzeb, or no ?
Officer : As yet
The battle's in the balance. Our troops
Swarm at the walls like flies, and Aurungzeb
Is where they cluster thickest.
Dara : It chafes me horribly
To be a-tented and the field so hot.
But to be generalled by him is worse
Than to return to Agra.
Oh ! Oh ! what devilish fate
Spies out on me to damn me.
Aurungzeb
To triumph where I've failed !
Let it not be, O God ! Think you
That he can beat the Persians ?
Officer : He has more men, more guns, more everything
Than you had, and by what you did not do,
He measures what he may.
Dara : That is the acutest prick of it,
That on my illness his success should mount,
And ride it to my shame.
(*Noise off.*)
Quick, quick,
Out and return. That noise
Frights me with what it bodes.
(*Exit* Officer)
Why did Jahan send me to Kandahar
To do the impossible, while Aurungzeb

Bores in my father's favour, and when
My trick is played to its foregone, fatal accomplishment,
He comes caparisoned like Providence,
To jump upon my lack, supplants me,
And with most hypocritical reluctance—
He would not, would not but to please Jahan
Have any hand in this—desires my pardon,
And leave but to obey, what he had fain
It had not been, his duty.

(*Re-enter* OFFICER)

What's toward ?

OFFICER : The Rajputs
With fiery valour mounting the Forty Steps
Have by the Persian musketeers been withered up,
Shooting at point-blank range. A scattered remnant
Is all that's left of them.

DARA : 'Tis well. 'Tis very well. The boy
Shall not out-siege me then. He must
Call off the assault, or loss
Pile upon loss. Oh God ! I had rather
The Persians should hold Kandahar for ever
Than Aurungzeb should take it.
Go out again, and mark
What's happening now.

(*Exit* OFFICER)

By how much more of troops,
Of horses, camels, and material,
That Shah Jahan hung thick on Aurungzeb,
By so much more shall his defeated honour
Droop under mine. Now on this base
I should be able to rebuild
My fallen reputation. How ? How ?
Soldiering's a coarse trade at best,
And subtle brains are wasted on it.
Better lay siege to men's intelligence,
And undermine at court. That's what I'll do.

(*Re-enter* OFFICER)

How stands the field?

OFFICER: Poorly indeed, as far as I can judge.
The Kandaharians smile behind their walls.

DARA: Praise be to God! Where's Aurungzeb?

OFFICER: He comes this way, as 'twere to seek your tent.

DARA: That cannot be. He would not
In the first flush and front of his disaster
Seek out his insulted brother.
He'll wait till after-thought has coloured it
With some excuse or other.

OFFICER (*looking out*): Nathless the prince is here. Shall I retire?

DARA: Do so, but be at call.

(*Enter* AURUNGZEB.)

Conqueror of Kandahar,
Though in your triumph I am doubly down,
I too will be a conqueror
Of mine own natural envy,
And in my "Well done, Aurungzeb,"
You'll hearing the shoutings of ten thousand "Well dones,"
Which shall greet you at Agra.

AURUNGZEB: You are not wont to be so witty, Dara,
But let the jest pass . . . I am stayed,
But not defeated, if I will it so.

DARA: What? Is Kandahar not yours?

AURUNGZEB: Have done. I tell you, mocking Dara,
I am thrust back, but still have men and guns
Enough to hack at Kandahar again,
And yet again.

DARA: And shall you do so?

AURUNGZEB: To what end? Our Mogul army
Is half a rabble, untrained, undisciplined,
Beside the Persians. We fight disorderly,
Shoot badly, while the Persian musketeers
Transfix the breasts they aim at.

Give me the power, the wherewithal, and time,
And I would forge this clumsy sword of Jahan's
Into a deadly weapon.
DARA : I had a worser one.
AURUNGZEB : We are both unlucky, brother.
And as for this o'erlording of your right,
It was not my desire.
Most willingly would I have served
Under your banner, but the king our father
Was absolute against it.
DARA : I am not in his favour.
AURUNGZEB : If I were in it, I shall not be now.
DARA : You may fare better in your next assault.
AURUNGZEB : I shall not make it.
The Persians are too strong for us,
And Kandahar's impregnable
Till we have better troops.
I have a soldier's eye, and what it tells me
My judgment must accept or fool itself.
The army's only had its edges frayed
By the to-day's attempt. Its centre's sound.
Why should I batter it to fragments
Against the stony brow of Kandahar,
When there is other work for't.
DARA : What do you mean by that ?
AURUNGZEB : I will be frank with you,
Though it be to my danger.
Men carry many faces through the world.
I speak not of false faces, but of true ones.
The innermost of the man
May baffle fine observance.
For me, I am something soldier, something
Of politician, courtier little,
But more than all these am I Mussulman.
The world—it grates me. Sooner would I spend
My life in praising God—renouncing

The temporal pomps of princes—than rule over
An empire doubling this.
DARA : It is well-known
That you are half a saint.
AURUNGZEB : If you were not a Sufi, Dara,
I'd have you king.
DARA : The throne's not vacant yet.
AURUNGZEB : It can be made so. You perceive my bent,
But not the arrow which I would let fly.
DARA : Not clearly. You keep in the shade.
AURUNGZEB : I'll step into the open. Shah Jahan
Uses the kingdom for a mason's tool,
Dips both his hands into the treasure box,
And like Aladdin raises every day
A palace, tomb, a temple, or a mosque
In mad profusion—every one
So rarely marbled, jewelled, wrought
With such immensity of labour that
Men can amaze no more, and God is shocked,
And the whole kingdom brought to the sharp
O' penury, and you, my brother,
Being the eldest and the properest heir,
Plundered to feed our father's vanity.
DARA : It is so, Aurungzeb, but we must wait
Till nature takes a hand.
AURUNGZEB : Nature—men are a part of nature,
And when she's slow can quicken her.
Mark too, Jahan flouts God,
And bids to Goa for a Christian priest,
Receives him honourably, and doth profess
An inclination—so my Mullah writes—
To be a Christian, to the which
The empress too inclines.
All this breeds murmuring rebellion
To Shah Jahan, and many
Wonder what Dara thinks.

DARA : That's
For Dara to determine when he knows
The scope and mettle
Of that which still is hid in Aurungzeb.

AURUNGZEB : I reach to my conclusion.
Go you in march to Agra,
Acquaint Jahan that Kandahar is ta'en.
That news will grace you in our father's eyes,
And he'll forget in his delight all fault
That he has taxed you with. Tell him
That Aurungzeb awaits in Kandahar
His more commands.
But I
Shall post haste after you, I and my army,
And on the rejoicing and unguarded city
Fall as a bolt from God.
Jahan shall be deposed, and Dara
Reign in his stead.

DARA : And Aurungzeb ?
Where is his profit, what does he expect
From Dara Shah ?

AURUNGZEB : Where is his profit *now* ?
Can he—can you go with bowed head
To Shah Jahan,
Say : " Please you, we have failed at Kandahar,
The city was too strong.
We would an if we could "—and bear
With patience, laughter, jeers, and punishment,
Be told that the harem's our proper place,
And women's garments deck our bodies best.
Hell shall engulf me first.
But let me
Strike one blow that shall vindicate
My soldiership—and then,
Give me your leave to give myself to God.
I shall be satisfied. I swear by the Koran.

DARA : Nothing more ?

AURUNGZEB : Nothing, except
That you abjure your Sufi heresy.

DARA : I'm yours—that last condition
Convinces me of your sincerity.
I am a Sunni from this moment, Aurungzeb.

AURUNGZEB : Then swear.

DARA : By the Koran I swear.

AURUNGZEB : Be ready to depart
Within this hour for Agra.

DARA : It is speedy.

AURUNGZEB : It is necessary.
Peace be on you.

DARA : And on you.

[*Exit* AURUNGZEB.]

Holloa !

[*Re-enter* OFFICER.]

OFFICER : My prince

DARA : We set out for Agra
Within the hour.
Gather my escort.

[*Exit* OFFICER.]

Dara Shah . . . .
O cunning Aurungzeb,
Would I might see into your plotting soul.
The map is cloudy. What my course shall be
Let circumstance, not Aurungzeb, decree.

SCENE 3

AGRA. *The Hall of Private Audience.*

BAHLOL, HIRA BAI, *afterwards* SHAH JAHAN, MUMTAZ, JAHANARA, JAFAR KHAN, AURUNGZEB.

BAHLOL : Away ! Jahan
Comes momently.
HIRA BAI : Most sweet Bahlol—
BAHLOL : Ay, you are cunning, but I'll hear you not.
HIRA BAI : Most excellent Bahlol,
Here is a purse of gold.
BAHLOL : Quick then, what would you have ?
HIRA BAI : News, news.
BAHLOL : The devil's dead,
And women are grown kind.
HIRA BAI : Wretch ! would you play with me ?
BAHLOL : Most willingly I would,
If time and place were apt.
'Tis Aurungzeb you would have news of ?
HIRA BAI : Why did I give thee gold ?
Speak, does he live ?
BAHLOL : He lives, and he is well,
If it be well to live. He is a prisoner.
Jahan and Dara fell on him
Not two days' march from Agra.
'Twas a devised surprise. Poor Aurungzeb
Was ambushed utterly, who else
Had stolen on the city in the night,
And like a thief when everyone's abed,
Had put it in his pocket. 'Tis a sluttish jade,
This chance, that stalks the robber on his fell intent,
And gyves him from behind.
HIRA BAI : A curse on Dara !
'Twas he betrayed his brother to Jahan.

BAHLOL : Tut, tut. Betray !
The word smells not of rank.
Eunuchs and women, common folk, betray,
Not princes.
But Dara's your man now, not Aurungzeb,
Whose candle's out, while Dara's is relit.
He is the merchant for your women's gear
If you can tickle purchase.
HIRA BAI : For saying that
I'd give you bloody mouth.
BAHLOL : Back to the harem, wild cat !
I hear voices.
[*Exit* HIRA BAI. *Enter* JAHAN *and* MUMTAZ.]
JAHAN : How glad am I that this rebellious prince
Is not your son.
MUMTAZ : How glad am I, Jahan,
His mother's dead,
And that the heart is cold that would have broken
At this unfilial treachery of her womb.
JAHAN : Oh ! he shall die, or in a fortress pent,
Wither his youth to greyness, and go off
By inches to the grave.
MUMTAZ : Jahan, be merciful.
JAHAN : Kings have no room for mercy
When would-be kings strike at them.
Care you indeed for me,
When thus you counsel mercy ?
MUMTAZ : Oh, my love,
Remember ! Add not
To past guilts this.
JAHAN : It is not that I would, but that I must.
I am not bloody by my nature,
It is my office makes me so.
Who reaches *that* (*pointing to his seat*) and sits on it in peace,
Must set his teeth and do what horrid deeds

Lead to a crown and keep it,
Or be himself undone.
MUMTAZ : He is your son, Jahan.
JAHAN : Were he not
A son, a brother, nephew, uncle,
Some tie in blood,
The nearer the more dangerous,
I could be merciful, nay I would be.
But a king's kindred, Mumtaz, are his snakes,
That have the 'vantage of his bosom,
And from it draw the very power they use
To touch him deadly.
MUMTAZ : Need it be always so ? Must kings,
To be kings, practise
What they abhor in their may-be successors,
And gazing their own deeds as in a glass,
Find them now hideous,
Which in themselves were pardoned by success.
Oh, for my sake, Jahan,
Break once this endless chain of violence,
And if it must be that you punish Aurungzeb,
Let it be like a father.
JAHAN : I would not have thee otherwise than tender,
My gentle lady.
MUMTAZ : You have sworn
That I am part of you, but of my gentleness,
Which you commend, you'll have no part.
Like to a sullen keeper of a door,
Which half is closed, half open, is your breast,
And I am strangered in the heart of me.
JAHAN : No, no, not by my heart
But by my judgment, and then only
On this one point, whereon if I'm not firm,
Myself, my crown, my queen,
I give to jeopardy. I know my Aurungzeb.
He's dangerous and subtle. Fate

Has played him to my rod and I must use it,
Or fool the engine.

MUMTAZ : Pray that a heart a wife may soften not,
A daughter may.

[*She lifts a curtain and* JAHANARA *enters.*]

JAHAN : Jahanara.

JAHANARA : My father.

JAHAN : Aurungzeb's not your brother, Jahanara,
For he's no longer son of Shah Jahan,
Nor can his false heart be akin to thine,
Which is so sweet and true.
Think not, weep not, for him,
A stranger to us both.

MUMTAZ : Your father, dearest, is indeed a king,
For he can with a word untie
The bonds of blood, command
Affection, memory, nature herself,
To give themselves the lie :
Forget the very name of Aurungzeb
That trembles on your lips.

JAHANARA : My father,
When your dear queen cannot with you prevail,
How then should Jahanara ?
I cannot, cannot plead for Aurungzeb.
I have no words, no policy,
That you should listen to me.
I do not understand this cruel world,
Nor men, nor why they do that that they do,
But if my brother is cast out from it,
I do beseech you, let me go with him.
If to a prison, there to sister him,
Until he needs no sister ; if to die,
To stay him to the last ; and then,
To mourn him in a still retreat with God,
And love and pray for you, and for your queen,
Till my poor light is spent.

Grant, oh grant, my father,
The petition of the humble Jahanara.

JAHAN : What then,
Wouldst leave Jahan for Aurungzeb—
Your father for a traitor ?
What is this love of women that it loves
When love itself bids cease ?

MUMTAZ : Women's love, Jahan,
Cannot be so divided from itself.
'Tis not a thing of fractions, but entire,
And what it is, it is.

JAHANARA : My father has his queen.
My brother—only himself, which is his enemy,
And God—and Jahanara.

MUMTAZ : His ears are stopped, he'll not be pitiful.
Come, Jahanara,
We'll take our sorrows with us.

JAHAN : Remain. Remain, I say,
And note
What I will do with Aurungzeb.
Bahlol,
Admit my minister and Aurungzeb.

[*Exit* BAHLOL.]

They wait without to hear my will on him.

[*Re-enter* BAHLOL, *followed by* JAFAR KHAN *and* AURUNGZEB.]

Is this the man I sent to Kandahar ?

JAFAR : He is the same man, majesty.

JAHAN : How different are these sames ! Is this the man
Who set forth to grasp honour,
And missing it, has fallen ; or a wily
And desperate conspirator, who creeps
Upon his belly to suspectless treason.
You are silent, Aurungzeb.
What think you you deserve at the king's hands ?

AURUNGZEB : Let the king say.

JAHAN : The king has but one answer,
To black rebellion—death.
[*A cry from* JAHANARA.]
I said the king—the father
O'ersways the king, and pardons you.
Nay more, he gives you
Scope to redeem
Your honour and your generalship.
Reduce the turbulent Deccan
To order, to which end
I make you viceroy.
For the rest,
The future is your servant,
And if your stark and most ambitious spirit
Must plot—be it to foil
Mine enemies.
The Deccan calls you—go.

AURUNGZEB : I thank you—God is great,
And if it be His pleasure, I shall serve
Both Him and you.
[*Exeunt* AURUNGZEB *and* JAFAR KHAN.]

JAHAN : Pious to the last.
Well, well, my queen,
And you, my daughter,
Are you contented with your Shah Jahan ?

MUMTAZ : Contented—proud,
That you have kinged your anger and your fear,
Base favourites of monarchs.

JAHAN : Nay, they are queened, not kinged—and Jahanara
Pays me with silence—ah, dark Aurungzeb,
Thou hast indeed a sister !

END OF ACT II.

ACT III

Scene i

Agra. *The Hall of Public Audience.* Jahan *and* Mumtaz *on their throne, which occupies a decorated niche in the centre, back.*

Shah Jahan, Mumtaz, Jafar Khan, Dara, Father Buseo, The Mullah, Bahlol, Page to Mumtaz, *afterwards a* Messenger.

Jahan : Can Aurungzeb write nothing but demands
For gold ? For gold. And still for gold !
What did we send him to the Deccan for ?
To be a sieve for gold ? a drain
Perpetual on our treasury ? The Deccan,
Which should enrich us, beggars us.
Are there not peasants, soil, sunshine and rain,
In the Deccan as elsewhere ? Has God
Laid his curse on it, so that men
Cannot be made to work, nor crops to grow,
No taxes to be levied on the crops,
And is a viceroy's function but to whine
For gold ? And then,
More gold to follow. Is this his gratitude
For that I pardoned him—nay, more than pardoned him,
Invested him with state ?

Jafar : It was most royal, majesty.
And yet—if I may venture——

Jahan : Venture—am I a tyrant
That you should preface what you will to say
That you deem just by " venture ? "

If you would commend Aurungzeb,
And so out-weigh my censure, do it, Jafar.
When you shall find I stop my ears with pride,
Then you be dumb—not else.

DARA : Old Jafar pauses. It baffles him
To find within the shrunken bag he carries
Of good conceits for Aurungzeb,
An odd one left.

JAFAR : Prince Dara,
Grudge not that while you bask you here at court,
In your great father's favour,
Aurungzeb,
Afar in the wild, difficult Deccan,
Has still a voice—not indeed to defend him,
For that I would not do—but to urge
What truth and reason
May drop in the other scale.

MUMTAZ : Good Jafar.

DARA (*aside to* THE MULLAH) : A partisan of Aurungzeb.

JAFAR : The Deccan
Was, as your majesty well knows,
For a whole generation torn by war,
The peasants pillaged, fields laid waste,
And what was smiling plenty suffered
Return to rankest jungle.
Then came a withered peace, the which
Was leaner made by flat incompetence,
Authority
Stealing the little that there was to steal,
And hoarding to his surfeit. Aurungzeb
Comes to all this, and cannot in a year
Change so much foul to fair. He must have time.

JAHAN : He shall have time.
We do not stint him time.
We'll give him twenty years in the Deccan.
His absence is our pleasure.

But in his messages he asks not time,
But gold. Throughout our reign,
And Jahangir's, gold, gold, nothing but gold
Has flowed to the Deccan, but from it
Not a rupee.

DARA : Aurungzeb increases daily, so they say,
His army, with pretence
To awe his neighbours, and has built
A capital, which with braggart impudence
He calls Aurungabad. Have viceroys
Capitals called after them ?

JAHAN : Is it for that we pardoned him,
That we should have another Shah Jahan,
And twin our glories with usurping Aurungzeb ?
But we must clip him. Is it not enough
That even we must think a little
To level up our treasure to our needs ?
Bebadal Khan
Still wants for jewels for our peacock throne.
Six emerald pillars only finished yet,
And six to do. I tell you, Jafar,
I'll empty all the mines of India,
And add to these the thousand rarest gems
That can be purchased in the marts o' the world,
Ere I will lack a jewel to complete
The throne we'll sit on. Touching Aurungzeb,
He shall be roundly answered.

DARA : He is ambitious,
And very cunning,
Conceives the pardoning of his traitorous action,
Which—praise to God—I was some aid to counter,
As it conferred an universal permit
To arrogate unchecked.

MUMTAZ : His headstrong youth
Must plead for him. I crave, Jahan,
For Father Buseo hearing.

JAHAN : We would not for the world deny it, love.
You have made converts, Father, have you not ?

BUSEO : A few, your majesty,
Have seen the light and entered in the fold.
Many more
Have seen the light, but tread not yet the way.
And that the light may brighter shine in Agra,
The emperor's sanction to erect a chapel
Wherein the Christian worship may be held,
I beg be granted.

MULLAH : The Mussulmans, majesty,
The most devoted and most numerous
Of all your subjects,
Pray you to tell this priest
He goes too far, insults them and the Prophet,
By his audacious asking. God
Will punish us, if he has way in this.

DARA : The Portugals
Are devil-taught. They and the English
Subdue the sea, which is the devil's land,
And by their most unholy magic,
They would change Mussulmans to devils too.
My voice is with the Mullah.

BUSEO : Thus do the powers of darkness
Testify to the light by fearing it.
Think ye his majesty invites me hither
To then deny me function ? But I rest
Upon his majesty's word.

MUMTAZ : My lord,
You have enquired into the Christian teachings,
And found much to commend in them.
These Christians are meek, of good report,
Speak truth, act kindly, tender and faithful are
Unto their single wives, abhor
All that's unseemly in the sight of God,
And honour kings. You shall advantage

Yourself and people by allowing them
The self-same freedom you accord to others.

JAFAR : The empress
Has not considered how the people
Are like to murmur at a Christian chapel
Flung in their very faces in the city.

JAHAN : Have I not said
That till I find the one and true religion—
If there be such to find—
All shall have play in my dominions,
My subjects choice of any God they will.
Have I myself not builded mosques and temples,
And shall I now deny
The Father one poor chapel ?
I will not. Your request
Is granted, Buseo. Jafar
Shall have the sanction duly drawn and sealed,
That none may question of it.

BUSEO : God's blessing on the king.

MULLAH (*aside to* DARA) : The empress
Is the king's vice. She is
Our enemy and the Prophet's.

DARA : That's most certain.

[*Enter a* MESSENGER.]

JAHAN : You are from Chitor.
What message do you bring from Jagat Singh ?

MESSENGER : The Rajah, majesty,
Did with an ostentatious ceremonial
Address the ramparts which engirdle Chitor
As thus :
" The mighty Shah Jahan
Commands you fall and crumble,
In that you were not builded with his leave."
Then to me turning :
" Tell your master
I have conveyed his most illustrious order

Unto my city's walls,
And yet you see
The walls remain. What can I do
With recreant walls that will not budge an inch
At word of Shah Jahan? Carry to him
My service and regret."

JAHAN: An insult from the Rajah Jagat Singh!
A puny Rajah insults Shah Jahan!
Thus Kandahar, thrice damnéd Kandahar,
Has repercussion. Jahangir,
Who conquered Chitor, and upon the conquered
Laid this condition, that unfortified
Chitor remain, shall not in's death be flouted,
Nor Jahan in his life. I'll to the field (*rises*)
In my own person. Jagat Singh
Shall jest no more, but be one.

MUMTAZ: I will accompany thee (*rises*).

JAHAN: Haste, love, is the essential of our purpose,
And all our usual pomp and tented splendour
Shall this occasion lack. I would not have thee
Campaign so roughly. Do thou stay at court,
And be my welcome home. Chitor
Is not a Kandahar, nor Jagat Singh
The Persian army. If within two weeks,
This Jagat is not crawling at my feet,
His country waste, his capital ungirt,
Call me a boaster and forget me, queen,
Unworthy of my arms.

MUMTAZ: Nay, nay, do not so proudly put me off,
Nor deem my body tender as my love,
That haste and roughness fright it. I will be
As careless of all comforts as yourself,
Ride at your pace, and be content with less
Than any of your soldiers. Indeed, indeed, Jahan,
I will be your companion, not your trouble,
And when you would have only men about you,

I will not mar your business. Sure there'll be
Some hour when you would say : " Would she were here,"
And that shall be my hour to steal upon you,
The only hour that I'll be a woman,
And doff my manly bravery, which else
Shall be my constant wear. It is most fit
The queen be left behind. Myself shall leave her,
When I set out with you.

JAHAN : And so you shall.
Hear ye then all !
On the Prince Dara we depend our power
Whiles we are absent, lending him
Such attributes of kingship as suffice
To fill the occasion's need. For us,
We do abridge our audience at this point.
Sunrise to-morrow sees us on the wing,
Too soon for that old braggart, Jagat Singh.

[*The Court rises.*]

SCENE 2

AGRA. *An ante-chamber to the apartments of the empress.*

AKBARABADI, FATHPURI, *afterwards* HIRA BAI, THE MULLAH, BAHLOL.

AKBARABADI : I am so weary I could yawn at love,
And be a wooden woman in his bed.

FATHPURI : The slumbery god is angry with us both,
And draws his purple bands around our eyes.
Yours are most visible, and mine
I'm sure are so to you.

AKBARABADI : Indeed they are. This watching on the queen
Will make us ill as she, but then
Ill with a difference. We should be only

Superfluous wives who might as well be dead,
As live neglected.

FATHPURI : Nay, we are dead
While Mumtaz lives.

AKBARABADI : If she should die . . . .

FATHPURI : Didst note
The physician's aspect when he left her sleeping ?

AKBARABADI : Nothing
Or good or bad that I could read in it.

FATHPURI : Methought
'Twas rather grave than solemn, as if
The issue was in balance.

AKBARABADI : It is most strange
If God should let her live. 'Tis said
That she is half a Christian in her heart,
And would not see the Mullah when he came,
After that father Buseo had been welcomed,
Who left with her the figure of a man,
Half-naked on a cross, that Christians worship.

FATHPURI : It is a sin to worship anything
That man has fashioned.

AKBARABADI : Perhaps 'twill bring God's vengeance on us all
For tending such an one.

FATHPURI : We did not choose our trouble.
She must forsooth ride forth with her Jahan,
Campaigning like a common trull, who hangs
On soldiers' heels to ply them in the camp,
And substitute their lawful mistresses.

AKBARABADI : It is a most improper thing to do
For high-born ladies. It is God's judgment
That she fell sick.

FATHPURI : Jahan, they say,
Had like to have unsworn his oath,
To reduce Chitor in half a month of days,
And trailed ingloriously to Agra back
Because his queen was sick—a pretty tale

To have writ of a Mogul conqueror,
And emperor of the world, great Shah Jahan
To turn and flee because his queen was sick !
But this would be her shame, and of her pride
Persuades him to the semblance of himself,
And he goes on—she and her fever
Unloads on us—we must o'erwatch ourselves,
And stain our faces with a long fatigue,
Because the queen is sick—and now she sleeps,
And yet we must not sleep.

AKBARABADI : I would I were as wide-eyed and awake
As is my hate of her.

FATHPURI : And I. Have we not cause to hate her ?

[*Enter from the inner chamber* HIRA BAI.]

What's the matter. Is the queen—— ?

HIRA BAI : The queen is as she was. There is no change.
Do you go in to her. I have
A message from the Mullah. He seeks me here
With tidings.

FATHPURI : We'd hear them too.

HIRA BAI : You shall—but not
Till I have spoke the Mullah privately.

AKBARABADI : You're too high-handed with us, Hira Bai,
The youngest wife too.

HIRA BAI : If 'twere not
That it would rouse the harem, and might open
Eyes that are now fast shut, I'd nip your cheek,
And rive the air with squeals. Go in, you baby.

[AKBARABADI *and* FATHPURI *go in.*]

What is it in this night that makes it seem
As it would last for ever, and the dawn
As far off as my Aurungzeb ? Something
I feel that I must do, but know not what,
And yet I shall know soon.

[*Enter* THE MULLAH.]

MULLAH : Peace be on you, daughter.
HIRA BAI : And on you, peace !
MULLAH : Where are the other women ?
HIRA BAI : They watch within. They will not dare disturb
What is toward between us.
MULLAH : It will be brief. The queen's physician
Reports to Dara thus—
HIRA BAI : Reports to Dara ! What a bloody wound
Your saying that inflicts on Aurungzeb.
MULLAH : Think you of that to-morrow.
To-night think of the queen.
HIRA BAI : I do. Well, the physician
Reports to Dara—God
Doom him to some unutterable fate.
MULLAH : Amen !—This is the kernel
Of the physician's wisdom—when the queen
Wakes from her present sleep, it will be clear
Whether she'll live or no. It is the crisis,
On which her illness sways as on an edge,
To fall this side or t'other.
HIRA BAI : If she lives——
MULLAH : 'Tis Buseo's triumph. The malignant priest
Has poisoned her, and she
Poisons Jahan in turn, and Jahan's wives
Will be put off, and men will pity them.
God's will be done. He can ordain,
Being all-powerful, that she shall arouse
To health of soul and body.
HIRA BAI : Ay. He *can* ordain, as also
That she shall go off sleeping.
MULLAH : 'Twere better so, than that an evil
Which is but yet half-grown should be fulfilled
In the rank bloom of sin. I'll leave you now.
You are a pious daughter of the faith,
And it may be you yet shall serve the faith
In ways unguessed.

HIRA BAI : I will believe it.

[*Exit* THE MULLAH.]

In ways unguessed . . . .

[*She goes to the entrance of the inner chamber and calls very softly. Re-enter* FATHPURI *and* AKBARABADI.]

HIRA BAI : The queen—— ?

FATHPURI : Nothing.

AKBARABADI : She breathes
As easy as a child.

HIRA BAI : That's ominous of good. The fever
Had been more stubborn if it were more kind.

FATHPURI : Says the physician—what ?

AKBARABADI : Tell us, sweet lady.

HIRA BAI : Sweet lady ! Akbarabadi
Calls me sweet lady, and the Mullah
A very pious daughter of the Prophet.
I am as sweet as pious, and as pious
As I am sweet. The queen
Will never wake again.

FATHPURI : Does the physician say so ?
She does not look like death.

HIRA BAI : Physicians
Are fools and guessers. The empress will not wake
Because she must not.

AKBARABADI : You frighten me. Your eyes
Are strange and fearful. (*To* FATHPURI) Does she not frighten you ?

FATHPURI : Speak, Hira Bai. I am more frightened
Of silence than of speech.

HIRA BAI : What would you be,
The wives of Shah Jahan,
Or drabs without a name, a place, a station,
The scorn of women, fragments
Of what were once the lights of the harem,
Now quenched and dark ; crown jewels,

That sparkled on the temples of a king,
By fresh assay discovered to be paste,
And in the midden dropped, and the whole round
Of golden setting hers.

FATHPURI : Sooner I would not be,
Than be the thing you name.

AKBARABADI : Indeed, indeed,
'Twould bring our noble fathers to such shame
That they would kill us.

HIRA BAI : What is this Mumtaz but a Christian,
And what she is Jahan will be. Her cunning
Shapes him so subtly to the mould it wears,
That what she wills he in his own despite
Determines he'll become. But now
Her cunning lies all open to our will
In yonder chamber. Do you stay me here,
A little, oh a very little while,
And when I am returned, then beat your breasts
And wail—you shall have cause.

FATHPURI : What would you—— ?

HIRA BAI : Is it so difficult
To stifle her ? A cushion
Pressed on that face that would have damned Jahan
Will do the trick, and twin
The unhelped work of nature. I will not
Be long away, sweet women.

[*She goes in.*]

AKBARABADI : My heart
Is beating so, so sounding in my ears,
That you must hear it too. Do you not hear it ?

FATHPURI : 'Tis your excited fancy. Let's converse,
As if the minutes were like those that were,
And carry nothing that's not usual.
Indeed they do not, not for us, we are
Two women talking. Is there any news
Of Shah Jahan at Chitor ?

AKBARABADI : Something I've heard
That he has reached the city. What will he do
When he comes back to this ? She is
Now in her chamber. If she should wake
And struggle—listen ! I could shriek,
But that I dare not.

FATHPURI : Pray you, calm yourself. We must
Be very calm. The Prince Dara
Apes all the arrogance of Shah Jahan,
Would court the favour of all people, but
His temper mars his craft. You do not listen.

AKBARABADI : How long may one have's breathing stopped and live ?

FATHPURI : I cannot tell, not long.
You wander wildly.
I would not give a diamond in my necklace
For any chances of Prince Aurungzeb
To climb again to favour.

AKBARABADI : Oh, he's done.
And 'tis not to be marvelled Hira Bai
Is full of spleen, and envious and racked
With malices uncounted when her prize
Loses the lottery. Is that her step ?

FATHPURI : No. You conjure silence
Into a sound.

AKBARABADI : It is a dreadful silence. Do you not feel
That it is dreadful ?

FATHPURI : You make it so. It has no quality
But what we give it.

AKBARABADI : Nay, even as we speak, her hands
Press on that royal face. Her breath
Imprisoned fights as in a deep-dug grave,
Th'immovable earth betwixt it and the air,
And chokes in darkness.

FATHPURI : What of it ? Is not all dying
Astoppage of the breath ? You are distraught.

There. There. A child
Might not more toy with terrors. Pray remember,
That Mumtaz' breathing had choked all of us
Into a worser death above the earth
Than any that's below it.

AKBARABADI : Hush, oh hush!

FATHPURI : 'Tis Hira Bai.

AKBARABADI : God! God! God!

[*Re-enter* HIRA BAI.]

FATHPURI : You do not speak. What are you? You are like
The great doom himself. I am afraid.

AKBARABADI : Say that you have not done it.
It cannot be that you have done it.
It is a dream—we will
Leave her in God's hands. Yes, oh, yes.

HIRA BAI (*loudly*) : Bahlol! Bahlol! Bahlol!

BAHLOL (*entering*) : What is it, mistress?

HIRA BAI : Call the physician. Call Dara. Rouse the court.

BAHLOL : Is there such matter for it? Has the queen
Waked from her sleep?

HIRA BAI : The queen is dead.

AKBARABADI : No. No. Not dead. She raves, Bahlol.

HIRA BAI : Mumtaz Mahal is dead.
She passed
Even now as I looked on her.

BAHLOL : Mumtaz Mahal! . . . Is't possible? Jahan
Will roar the world. . . .
You are women, and can weep.
For me, this is a whisper
That I'll make thunder of.
The queen! The queen!

[*He rushes off.*]

HIRA BAI : Now, women, let's acclaim
A painted sorrow. Safety lies
In loud lamentings and in streaming eyes.

[*As they raise the wail for the dead the scene closes.*]

SCENE 3

AGRA. *A private apartment of the emperor.*

SHAH JAHAN, JAFAR KHAN, BAHLOL, *afterwards* JAHANARA.

JAHAN : Well—what do you want with me ?
JAFAR : To know if the king
To-morrow holds an audience. It is fourteen days
Since the late empress—upon whom be peace !—
Was funeralled with all fitting majesty,
And in that time
Nor court, nor people have looked on the king.
JAHAN : The king
Abides him with his grief. Tell them that Shah Jahan,
To whom the world pays court, is in his turn
The courtier of his grief, or if you will
Play dolorously with conceit, tell them
That Shah Jahan has wed another bride,
Whose sombre beauties do engage him wholly
In amorous toying, and her name
Is sorrow. Nay, tell them what you will,
So that you leave me and my grief together.
JAFAR : 'Tis reported, majesty,
That you are sick, a hundred rumours
Sweep through the city, and the people
Are much perturbed. To show yourself
Is the best answer.
JAHAN : Am I not sick then ? Sick in my very soul,
And never to be well—never—never—
The rarest and most exquisite of women,
The most enchanting spirit that did ever
Inform mortality—to be seen no more—
No more be heard—no more
Be thought on as she was, but as she is,
A memory—but as a memory

More potent than all else that lives and breathes.
Oh, how I hate all things that live and breathe,
And she does not. Prate you to me of kings,
And courts and people ?
They are nothing. The world
Has but one king, one subject,
Death and sorrow.

JAFAR : Pardon your servant, that he dares
To speak what's in him. You do lose
Yourself too wildly in this bitterness.
You are not a private man, but Shah Jahan,
And that Jahan was graced with a sweet queen,
Cannot be substance of so huge a grief
That it blots out the world.

JAHAN : It does, Jafar. I tell thee, man, it does.

JAFAR : Why then,
The world will blot out you.
The mighty Shah Jahan
Loses a wife, though he has many wives,
And in that loss is lost, himself and crown,
Though he has but one crown to lose withal.

JAHAN : What, what ?

JAFAR : Your sons
Dara and Shuja, Murad, Aurungzeb,
Will bloodily contest the throne
You throw to them. Akbar and Jahangir
Yielded to death their purple. You
Put it away with tears. Oh, I could weep
Myself into a dotage. Such a king
To ebb away in water !

JAHAN : Thou art a traitor, Jafar Khan, and here,
I dispossess thee of all dignities
That I have laid on you. Thou shalt learn
That I still wear a crown.
Bahlol ! (*Enter* BAHLOL.)
Order my guard.

JAFAR : I am content.
JAHAN : Bahlol,
Stay yet a moment.
Content ? You are content ?
JAFAR : Content that you are roused
From the deep lethargy in which I found you.
JAHAN : I see. (*He dismisses* BAHLOL *with a gesture.*) Ah,
Jafar,
You have not loved as I.
JAFAR : The Prophet
Bade husbands love their wives, and so I do,
But count them not so precious that they fill
The total orbit. Your majesty
Has other wives to love.
JAHAN : They are women, I have married them, and so
Let them be wives, but my harem
Is in my heart, and that
Was buried in the garden where she is,
Who was herself the garden of all women,
And bloom of earth. But this
Is not betwixt us. For that you have spoke,
And hurt me to my good, it was well done,
And to-morrow
We will hold audience, and as is our wont
Upon the balcony we'll show ourselves,
And shame the face of rumour. One thing mark,
And bring to action most immediately.
JAFAR : It shall be marked and done.
JAHAN : This Father Buseo. I do revoke
All privileges soever I have granted
To him and to the Christians. Him I banish.
The God that mv dear consort so much favoured
Is a false God. All Gods are false,
And cheat their trusters,
And there is but one answer to all questions—
The grave. Hence. Hence. My grief

Is now again in spate. Speak no more word
But go. To-morrow
I will be Shah Jahan. To-night
The outcast of all comfort, torn
Upon the nails and spikes of memory.

[*Exit* JAFAR KHAN. *Enter* JAHANARA.]

JAHANARA : You sent for me, my father.

JAHAN : Did I send ? I had forgot.

JAHANARA : You would be alone ?

JAHAN : From the world, yes. But you
Are not the world. The daughter of a mighty king,
Yet of so gentle and so meek a spirit,
That even glory is by you abashed,
And doubts his lineage.

JAHANARA : A lowly spirit well becomes the lowly,
And such am I.
Would it ease your heaviness, good sir,
To speak your grief, or shall I
Be near you, touch your hand,
And weep with you in silence ?

JAHAN : Be near me, yes. For tears,
All I had fell in a swollen rush
When I looked on her face.

JAHANARA : There was no fever in it. Still and pale and calm,
As one who passed in peace.

JAHAN : She took it with her
Into her grave. Who henceforth would find peace
Must seek it there.

JAHANARA : Do they not say that sorrow
Which broods upon itself becomes
The shame of sorrow—which is bitterness.

JAHAN : How 'scape we this inbreeding ? When was it
That I chastised the Rajah of Chitor ?
And brought him to his knees, nay, nay, not when,
But who—who crashed the walls of Chitor ?
He was a soldier. Who think'st thou

Builded the Palace wherein now we mourn,
For that it holds no more the light of it,
Who on the barren and bare earth that was,
Whereon we tread, with a magician's spell,
Caused it to rise in arch, and wall and tower,
And doméd copy of the bending sky,
And lo ! 'twas Agra—wonder of all cities.
He was indeed a piler-up of splendours.
But who did this—not I. Know you who did it, child ?

JAHANARA : My father jests with me. He may forget
The name of Shah Jahan, the world will not.

JAHAN : You have said it. The world *shall* not.
That Shah Jahan, the Shah Jahan who loved
A living woman I do put away.
A new Jahan abiding with her memory,
Which he'll entomb with a perpetual glory,
Succeeds him at the instant. I am big
With grandiose conception.

JAHANARA : What moves you, father, to this sudden start ?

JAHAN : Never has queen or woman been so loved,
And never shall one be so sepulchred.
Over her ashes I'll erect my masterpiece,
And ages following when they gaze upon't,
Dazzled and faint with beauty, they shall murmur
The names of Mumtaz and of Shah Jahan.

JAHANARA : Nay, my father,
Your own heart is her noblest monument.

JAHAN : What say you, Jahanara ?
Of Jaipur marble and sandstone from Fatehpur,
Red as her lips, it shall be builded.
Each block cut perfectly, with not an edge
That is not sharp and true, part unto part so fitted,
That it shall seem as if the building grew
As life were in't. The crown of it,
A dome so aerial and fantastically light,

That Samarkand's most cunning masons shall not
Believe their hands have raised it.
For the bedecking of this cloud-beaming sepulchre
The earth shall be my jewel-box.
Its costliest gems and rarest stones I'll rifle,
And they immortally shall flash their splendours
For her who was the jewel of the world,
And is its loveliest sorrow.

JAHANARA : You are as one entranced. Sir—sir—
You lose touch of the earth, but not
The dust that's of it.

JAHAN : Every land
Shall pay its tribute to her. Jade and crystal
Shall be the grief of China. The Punjab
Shall weep in jasper, Bundelkund
In diamonds, Persia
Drop tears of onyx and of amethyst.
Even cold Tibet shall melt in turquoises.
Sapphires and lapis lazuli Ceylon shall drop,
And far Arabia shall her mourning show,
And sigh in coral and cornelian.
The heart of all, the cenotaph, whereunder
Her precious relics lie, shall be
Draped with a sheet of pearls, and have
Before't a screen of gold,
Be-starred with gems that shall out-star the sky,
And make it lack some lustre.

JAHANARA : Father! Jahan! You do o'ertop yourself
With these imaginings. Why do you stare so?

JAHAN : It is before me. See Jahanara! See
The Taj Mahal that shall be.

[*The chamber has darkened, and a distant vision of the Taj appears. It fades away, and the light returns.*]

Call Bahlol. I'll have
My architects. At once. At once. We'll plar
Even as the vision showed it. Ere the dawn
It shall be fixed on paper. I am afire.
The genius in me now must take command,
Or break the instrument. Bahlol! My architects!

[*As* BAHLOL *enters the scene closes.*]

END OF ACT III.

ACT IV

Scene i

Aurungabad. *A room in* Aurungzeb's *palace. A common soldier is on his knees before* Aurungzeb, *with an officer standing over him.*

Aurungzeb, Mir Jumla, Soldier, Officer, *afterwards* Hira Bai.

Aurungzeb (*to the officer*) : Is this the fellow
  Who sings and plays ?
Officer : 'Twas he your highness heard
  As you passed through the camp.
Aurungzeb : I would he were of rank, not common stuff,
  That I might show an ordinance of mine
  Shall not be broke by my near'st officer,
  And be unmeted by the penalty.
Soldier : Mercy, mighty prince. In the name o' God,
  I cry you mercy.
Mir Jumla : What has the fellow done ?
Aurungzeb : Done ! Vexed the sober ears
  O' the soldiers with his jigging foolery.
Mir Jumla : But that ! A merry soldier
  Is a good soldier. Your melancholy man
  Eats out his heart before the fight begins,
  And spreads his spleen about him like a cloud.
  Whip sadness if you will, not merriment.
Soldier : Mercy, mighty prince. In the name o' God
  I cry you mercy.

AURUNGZEB : I have forbidden
All music in my camp and in my house.
A soldier's business is to fight and pray,
And when the sword or musket's not in use,
Let him tell's beads upon his rosary,
As I do. We are God's soldiers, we,
And turn our arms upon His enemies.
For this musician, hang him on a tree,
And the wind play him like an instrument,
Till vultures make an end. Take him away.

[*Exit* OFFICER *with* SOLDIER.]

MIR JUMLA : Is this a mosque then, Aurungzeb, that I have come to ?

AURUNGZEB : If you will, Mir Jumla. I tell you,
I have at last fashioned an army
That is to that of Jahan's and my brothers,
Order to chaos, a goring bull
To sheep. With your artillery added,
A knife to carve up Asia.

MIR JUMLA : What are your last advices from the court ?

AURUNGZEB : Jahan grows impotent, Dara o'erswells, the people
Groan under burdens. The extravagant tomb
Jahan has builded over Mumtaz' ashes
Dips the scale 'gainst him almost to the bed.

MIR JUMLA : 'Tis said to be a marvellous piece of work.

AURUNGZEB : The stretched resources of a mighty empire
Concentred on a folly.
Four hundred lakhs of rupees, twenty thousand men,
And five years' labour. If Jahan
Has builded not his ruin on the Jumna,
I am not Aurungzeb.

MIR JUMLA : And for a woman. That
Sticks in my throat. A woman.

AURUNGZEB : No matter.
The board is set, Mir Jumla, and the game
Of empire starts afresh.

MIR JUMLA : 'Twill be a bloody one. Would it were possible
To know the end of it. Have you no man of stars
To read this script of fortune ?

AURUNGZEB : 'Twere impious so to do. God doth reveal Himself
Unto His servants. Has He not put
On each man His own mark, whereby the issue
That is in him's foretold ? If He has made
Jahan a madman builder and a lover,
My brother Dara in his own conceit
So muffled that he trips upon the hem of it,
Shuja unready when the action calls,
And Murad brainless, dissolute and brave,
Which bravery rushes on the spike of loss,
Is it not in His plan, part of His script
That you name fortune's. And if Aurungzeb—

MIR JUMLA : Why do you pause on Aurungzeb ?

AURUNGZEB : I am in pause, Mir Jumla, every way,
And action hangs on moment. Ha ! what's this ?

[*Re-enter* OFFICER.]

OFFICER (*handing* AURUNGZEB *a paper*) : A message from the emperor.

AURUNGZEB : The messenger ?

OFFICER : Would speak you private, meanwhile waits your pleasure.

AURUNGZEB : Tell him to wait it then.

[*Exit* OFFICER. AURUNGZEB *breaks the seal and reads the message.*]

So. So.

MIR JUMLA : What says Jahan ? An order
To visit him at Agra ? It is years
Since his affection gazed on Aurungzeb.
And Dara too, his brotherly love
Is hungered and would eat.

AURUNGZEB : It is you, Mir Jumla,
Jahan would have at Agra.

He orders you to leave upon the instant,
And—this is indeed great news——
Confers on you the office of prime minister.

MIR JUMLA : Impossible ! What then of Jafar Khan ?

AURUNGZEB : It seems that Jafar Khan
Urges that he is weary, and would drop
His public burdens. Read the paper.

MIR JUMLA (*reading*) : It is so. Prime minister of Shah Jahan.
This works out well. At Agra
I can do much.

AURUNGZEB : For whom ?

MIR JUMLA : Why do you ask ? For Aurungzeb.
Are we not leagued together ?

AURUNGZEB : I have enough of friends at court, Mir Jumla.
Jahan and Dara
Have made them for me, though they guess it not.
You and your guns
Will do us better service with me here,
Or with me there, but here or there
With me.

MIR JUMLA : And yet it may not be the properest policy
To disobey Jahan. This wants consideration.

AURUNGZEB : Prime minister of Shah Jahan—that's now.
Prime minister of Aurungzeb—that's not so certain,
And much to do before that hope matures.
Truly, you must consider.

MIR JUMLA : You cannot doubt me. I fix my hopes on you.
Jahan's throne totters. How should I then
Stay fortune on that cast ? If then I go——

AURUNGZEB : You will not go.

MIR JUMLA : Will not ? Will not ?

AURUNGZEB : Shall not.

MIR JUMLA : Whose " shall not," Aurungzeb,
Must I bow down to ? You are not
My emperor yet. A viceroy of the Deccan,
Out of his father's favour, with three brothers,

Of whom one's on the crest, and two
Less under than are you. I speak not thus,
Because I doubt or waver on the throw,
But that you leap from means to end, and from that end
Derive authority, which does not
Belong to means. Your absolute " shall not "
Anticipates too much.

AURUNGZEB : Mir Jumla,
I do not doubt you, long as you believe
The star of Aurungzeb, though still obscured,
Is destined to blaze forth the regnant star.
But court and office, Dara and Jahan,
May play strange tricks with faith, and Aurungzeb
Grow smaller when he's spied at from afar.
In a word, you are my prisoners,
You and your followers.

MIR JUMLA : Never. I will——

AURUNGZEB : You cannot go to Agra. I have seized
All ferries that do cross the Narbadā.

MIR JUMLA : Seized all the ferries——

AURUNGZEB : Every one.

MIR JUMLA : To what purpose ?

AURUNGZEB : To conceal from Dara and Jahan
The progress of events in the Deccan,
And to secure
My passage when the moment beckons me.

MIR JUMLA : But the messenger ?

AURUNGZEB : Was passed by my permission,
And his return's unlikely.

MIR JUMLA : The struggle then begins.

AURUNGZEB : It is the first move.

MIR JUMLA : I must e'en then connive at my arrest,
And be your willing prisoner. I had not deemed
That destiny was afoot. I am well pleased,
Though your " shall not " my pride must rankle at.

AURUNGZEB : 'Twill soon have stuff to feed it. A full stomach
Forgets its injuries. But I bethink me.
The messenger—here is some mystery—
Requests my private ear. Adieu awhile.

MIR JUMLA : Take care. A dagger thrust,
And Aurungzeb's no longer in the running.

AURUNGZEB : God orders all, Mir Jumla.

[*Exit* MIR JUMLA. *Re-enter* OFFICER.]

Inform the messenger from Shah Jahan.
That I await him.

OFFICER : Instantly, highness.

[*Exit* OFFICER. *A cloaked figure enters.*]

AURUNGZEB : What means the cloak ? How dar'st thou come disguised
Into my presence.

[*The figure throws aside the cloak, and reveals* HIRA BAI.]

The lady Hira Bai. Are *you* the messenger ?

HIRA BAI : I came with him.

AURUNGZEB : You came with him. Have you then fled the court ?

HIRA BAI : Aurungzeb, I have. Your face
Is full of question. Hear me then.

[AURUNGZEB *inclines his head.*]

While you, Aurungzeb, forgetting me,
To whom you have deeply vowed,
Have in the Deccan builded up your power,
I, I who cannot
Forget where I have loved, have secretly
Been as a cunning finger in that hand
Which has been yours at Agra. Day and night
I have thought and schemed for you.

AURUNGZEB : I thank you, lady, but I depend
On other aids than yours.

HIRA BAI : It was not so, proud Aurungzeb,
When you did oath your constancy to me,

And at my bidding, yes, at mine,
Forswore yourself in the cup. Ah, you remember that.

AURUNGZEB : If you were wise,
You'd have me not recall it. Fasting and prayer
Have cleansed me from that sin.

HIRA BAI : Saint Aurungzeb, so pure you are and near to God,
That in your shadow I would be cleansed too.

AURUNGZEB : From what ?

HIRA BAI : From murder. Ah, you start.
A Mogul prince starts at the very word.

AURUNGZEB : Woman, what have you done ?

HIRA BAI : Murdered for Aurungzeb—for Aurungzeb.
Come now, " I thank you lady." From your store
Of thank yous, have you not one
To throw at my famishing heart, for that I did
To profit in your cause—and God's,
A holy murder, Aurungzeb.

AURUNGZEB : Whose ? Whose ? Not, not Jahan.
No. No. Then Dara ? Rack me no longer. Speak.

HIRA BAI : Your enemy who banished you from Agra—
God's enemy—the friend of Christians—
Dara's friend—Mumtaz Mahal.

AURUNGZEB : She died of sickness. You are distract,
Or fool me to your purpose.

HIRA BAI : She died of a pillow, which I pressed upon her
As she lay sleeping.

AURUNGZEB : Is't possible ?

HIRA BAI : Most easy and most secret. You, Aurungzeb,
And Dara, and the Mullah, all of you
Would purge the court of Buseo, but could not.
I did it with a pillow.

AURUNGZEB : Why did you flee the court. To tell me this ?

HIRA BAI : Ungrateful Aurungzeb. The tale was blabbed
By a conniving bosom of Jahan's
When sinking to her end. The frightened wretch

On this confession passed. Oh may she rot
In spirit as in body! The good Mullah
Warned and secreted me. Jahan
In horrible rage, and foiled in's search of me,
Accounted all alike, and did
Upon his whole harem *my* vengeance wreak
More than his own, flinging his shrieking wives
To the royal elephants, whom their thunderous hooves,
Pent in a narrow den, as 'twere unknowingly,
Stamped to amorphous death. I, lying hid,
The occasion of the messenger presenting,
Crept out, and with contrivance of the Mullah
Made of his escort one. So Aurungzeb,
What will you do with me?

AURUNGZEB: I do not know. You are the wedded wife of Shah Jahan.

HIRA BAI: The wife of Shah Jahan, whom Aurungzeb
Loved wildly once. Say that you love me still.
And if it be the throne you strike for's yours,
And that I may not share it—if that dream
Is dreamed and over—yet if I share you,
Ah Aurungzeb, I'll wear a happier crown
Than empery can have. Wilt put it on my brow?
Sure—sure this coldness cannot
Be your true wear. The heart I knew and loved
Beats in you yet. It must do so, it must,
Or you are perjured to the top of hell,
And I the most deceivéd of all women,
And—mark you—Aurungzeb,
The most desperate.

AURUNGZEB: You are a tiger,
Changing from feline purr to snarling rage.
My house is not a jungle, nor am I
Your hunter. Listen.
The splendid temple of Kēsava Dēva
I have levelled to the dust. The dancing girls,

The sacred minions of their filthy gods,
I have disbanded, and forbidden
On pain of death to ply their amorous trade
On any ground I rule. Shall I do this,
In service of my God and of His Prophet,
And clip an undivorced and flying wife
To my allegiance. The heady youth
Your beauty snared, and his immortal soul
Drew to the verge of th' pit, is not this Aurungzeb.
Go where you will, you shall not go with me.

HIRA BAI : Now, Hira Bai, be yourself, and strike
This liar to the earth.

[*She draws a dagger and attempts to stab* AURUNGZEB, *who—not unprepared for something of the sort—seizes her wrist and the dagger drops.*]

AURUNGZEB : It is not my fate.

[*The* OFFICER, *hearing the noise enters.* HIRA BAI *has sunk to the ground and is sobbing violently.*]

AURUNGZEB (*to the* OFFICER) : I did not call.

OFFICER (*retiring*) : Pardon, highness.

AURUNGZEB (*to* HIRA BAI, *pointing to the dropped dagger*)
There is the key
That must unlock your end, not mine.
Your own hand do't, and quickly.
This is a timeless parting.
For Aurungzeb, a coffin or a crown !
For you—poor wretch—the dice is thrown and down !

[*He goes out.* HIRA BAI *slowly stretches out her hand towards the dagger as the scene closes.*]

Scene 2

Agra. *The Hall of Private Audience.*

Shah Jahan, Dara, *afterwards* Jafar Khan, Messenger

Shah Jahan : What keeps Mir Jumla. My peremptory order
Demanded him at Agra. Has Aurungzeb
Infected him with disobedience ?
Dara : Why did he go to Aurungzeb at all ?
Jahan : His way of march. Moreover,
He will observe, and of his observations
Make full report.
Dara : It may be
Your orders reached the eyes of Aurungzeb,
And not his tongue.
Jahan : If I thought that—but no, he durst not.
Dara : Aurungzeb waxes large in the Deccan,
And what his pride durst not, his spleen and jealousy
May prick him to.
Jahan : Mir Jumla's fastened tightly to my service
By favours past and future—I'll not doubt him.
Here's Jafar Khan to irk me.
[*Enter* Jafar Khan.]
Jafar : Majesty.
Jahan : What is't ? I know you are agog
To leave your master. You shall find me
A not ungrateful one, and your retirement
Shall be a plenteous and a pleasant resting
From the heaviness of office.
Jafar : Whate'er you do you cannot otherwise
Than do imperially.
Jahan : I but await the arrival of Mir Jumla
To set you free. Till then,
We'd have you stretch your duty a little further
Than your desire would have it.

JAFAR : My desire
Outruns my duty, like an untired youth
A sick companion.

DARA : Your duty sick ? That's a strange term. Why sick ?

JAFAR : Your pardon, prince, if I don't answer that
Save to my master.

JAHAN : Answer me then, Jafar.

JAFAR : I'm sick because your kingdom, Shah Jahan,
Is a sick kingdom.

DARA : Who make it so then ? Councillors
Who traffic with the emperor's enemies,
Sedition breeders, hiding them at court
In habits of fair outward honesty,
But lined within with guile.

JAFAR : I am not touched. The king
Knows how I have served him, and if he
Had served his people half as well, he would not
Be heir of what he is—a million curses !

DARA : This in the king's hearing !

JAHAN : Calm yourself, Dara. Treason
Shows smilingly—this ugly face
Is confessed honesty, which has no tricks
To ogle whom she favours. Jafar Khan
Has ever had the freedom of his lips,
And truth to tell has used that freedom freely,
As now he shall. A million curses !
All kings are cursed
Because they are kings and rule,
And every over-man in narrowing state
Is cursed by those below. What is it, Jafar,
That your sick duty, ere it yields the ghost,
Would say to Shah Jahan ?

JAFAR : Look on your kingdom, majesty.

JAHAN : Let us look on't together, Jafar.
(*Taking him to the balcony*)
There is my kingdom, there beyond the Jumna,

Beneath that dome that floats upon the air,
As lotus bud on water. There my soul
Sits on his throne of sorrow with his queen,
And holds his court with worms.

JAFAR : Awake, Jahan, awake, O king,
And sleep no more with shadows.
Let the imperial sepulchre you have raised
Fulfil the office of her memory,
And tell to wondering time her grace and virtue.
Do you attend the living. Your wretched subjects,
O'ertaxed, oppressed, cry out their misery
To their unanswering lord. They ask for bread,
You give them literal stone. Are palaces and tombs
The stay of gnawing stomachs ?

JAHAN : Gnawing stomachs ! Either your words
Do much o'erhang the edges of the truth,
Or I am badly served. You, Dara,
Who whiles I have walked aside with melancholy,
And strove with my hurt spirit,
Have worn my power, reply to Jafar Khan.

DARA : Words against words. Let me reply
In action—that's a dungeon for this man,
Who with presumption riding on past service,
And his notorious dislike of me,
And secret favour to false Aurungzeb,
Traduces all of us.

JAFAR : Oh, my dear master, be not flattered thus.
Prince Dara has but postured in your glass,
Which never has been turned to the big world
That lies without the court, on which nathless
The pomp and glory of your state is founded.
If that is rotten, all else is a sham,
Like to a painted face upon a harlot.
Ride out upon the common ways with me,
And you shall meet your anti-emperor.
He,

With withered hand and glazéd eye, stalks forth,
And wins your subjects from you.
If that's your kingdom on the Jumna there,
Where beauty is and hallowed graciousness,
The Lord of Hindostan's not Shah Jahan,
But Famine, and his train
Is beasts that once were men.

JAHAN : That *are* men, Jafar. But complete your picture
And tint it as you will, we'll look on it,
So that your brush be truth not artistry.

JAFAR : I limn no picture, majesty. These things
Bleed through the flux of words, and would be seen,
Though sight be maiméd by them. Life itself
Is offered for a loaf, and goes a-begging.
Rank would be freely given for a cake, yet none
Would buy it at so desperate a cost.
Dogs' flesh is now become a luxury.
The dead are dug from graves, and their bones pounded
To eke the flour that's sold.
Nay, men eat men, and a son's flesh
Is dearer to his father than his love.
The roads are massed with corpses, and who still
Are miserable enough to be alive,
Wander with vacant air from place to place,
And want the strength to cure themselves with death.

JAHAN : What emperor rules plagues ? I send them not.
These men have gods, and priests, and prayers.
Perchance
The priests are lazy, and the prayers too few.
'Tis ever thus.
Kings must make good the offences of the gods,
Or lose their credits. But content you, Jafar,
We'll stir ourselves in this.

[*Enter a* MESSENGER.]

You are in haste
To drop your tidings.

MESSENGER : Khalīlullah Khan
Acquaints your majesty that Prince Aurungzeb,
With battle-fronted army,
Has crossed the Narbadā.

DARA : He is disclosed ! The traitor is disclosed !
He, majesty, has replied
To Jafar Khan.

JAHAN : No more of that. I'll stake
My crown on Jafar's faithfulness. This news
Sinks other matters to the secondary.
Now Aurungzeb has ta'en the fatal step,
Deleting all consideration more
That fatherhood may tender—'tis too much
That I have tendered—from this moment
He is mine enemy, and shall be crushed
To the remorseless stop.

DARA (*to* MESSENGER) : Know you aught
Or do you aught conjecture of Mir-Jumla ?

MESSENGER : He is with Aurungzeb.

JAHAN : Oh, 'tis monstrous
That treason should have such a magnet in it,
That from their centres other loyalties
Are torn away and wrecked.
Where is Khalīlullah Khan ?

MESSENGER : He's falling back as Aurungzeb advances.

JAHAN : To you, Dara,
I entrust my uttermost strength
To chastise Aurungzeb. Oh, let him feel
Once more the iron of defeat. His person
Take if you can, and bring him,
A traitor for the second time before me,
'Twill be his last. For me,
I am not what I was ; must be contented
To hear not act the story.

DARA: He was my insolent at Kandahar,
And I will rid the empire of this rat,
Or tail him squeaking to the gaze of you.

JAHAN: Summon the generals, Dara, to a council,
And food and sleep bestow on this brave officer,
Who has ridden fast and long. I will recall
Forgotten tricks of soldiership, that shall give you
The pull o' the field. No hurry, but
An ordered quickness govern everything.

[*Exeunt all except* JAFAR KHAN.]

JAFAR: O Mumtaz, thou who shared his rule in life,
In death possess him wholly. What he is
Scarce nods acquaintance with the man he was.
My heart must serve him still. My judgment
Deserts unwillingly to Aurungzeb,
And does so shame me that I cast it off
And will not use it more.

[*He follows the king.*]

SCENE 3

AGRA. *The Hall of Public Audience. The Peacock Throne has been completed and occupies the centre niche.*

THE MULLAH, BAHLOL, *afterwards* SHAH JAHAN, JAFAR KHAN, JAHANARA, AURUNGZEB, MIR JUMLA, OFFICERS, *etc. of* AURUNGZEB.

MULLAH: What's the matter, Bahlol?
Where are the thronging courtiers of Jahan,
The soldiers, guards, the ladies,
The people seeking justice of their lord,
This is a court day, is it not?

BAHLOL: Ay, 'tis the day. As for the courtiers,
You herald them—they will be here anon.

But they are bloody and must wash themselves
Before they come to court. 'Twould be unseemly else.

MULLAH : Strange revolutions God has worked, Bahlol.

BAHLOL : With help of men—and something
Of a most excellent elephant.

MULLAH : God has His instruments—a common fly
May serve God's purposes—but
An elephant—how mean you ?

BAHLOL : Why, 'twas an elephant that ruined Dara,
And scattered his great host.

MULLAH : Riddle me not, my good Bahlol,
Or save my brain and tend the answer too.
An elephant—not Aurungzeb
Defeated Dara ?

BAHLOL : I will tell you
What I have heard—and on authority
Of one on the field at Samūgarh,
Where Aurungzeb and Dara shocked together.
The battle hung
On a pin's point. Dara on's elephant
Was mark for the enemy's fire, and was persuaded,
For safety of his all-important person,
To come down from his howdah,
And mount a horse. Mark, now, how slight a thing
Tips the great world.

MULLAH : A eunuch a philosopher !

BAHLOL : Why not ? All men have mistresses,
And the poor eunuch,
Denied his nature, couples with philosophy,
Who bears strange children by him.
No sooner did the army of Prince Dara
Observe the empty howdah, than arose
The cry : " Dara is dead." In vain
The horsèd Dara strove to show himself.
" Dara is dead," " the prince is dead," ran through
The dismayed ranks, whereon

The enemy pushed him home, and huge disaster
Fell on th' imperial cause—but that
All Agra knows.
They say
The people welcomed Aurungzeb as if
He was their idol. I heard the shouting.

MULLAH : It was so. And is this emptiness
The court of Shah Jahan ?

BAHLOL : A eunuch more or less, old Jafar Khan,
Who had no legs to run with all the others
To greet and fawn on Aurungzeb,
That is the train of my magnificent master.

MULLAH : It is God's judgment on an unbeliever.

BAHLOL : I hope that Aurungzeb remembers me,
And how I served him when he was a prince,
And hated Dara—lives he or is he prisoner
This Dara ?

MULLAH : He is in flight, a wretched remnant
Of his immediate followers with him.

BAHLOL : Where are the Princes Shuja and Murad ?

MULLAH : They advance each from their separate kingdoms,
Shuja from Bengal, Murad from Gujerat,
Towards Agra.

BAHLOL : To contest with Aurungzeb. They are too late.
He's in the centre, but there still will be
Some pretty blood-letting before all's done,
And Aurungzeb's unbrothered. It is not safe
For emperors to have brothers.

MULLAH : No, nor sons either.

[*A roll of drums is heard faintly.*]

BAHLOL : That's Aurungzeb.

MULLAH : I will retire. This all-deserted palace
Appals me.

BAHLOL : A riderless elephant—remember that.

MULLAH : 'Tis a tale
Not likely to please Aurungzeb, whose prowess

It something takes from—*you* remember that.
[*Exit* THE MULLAH.]

BAHLOL: Bahlol, you are a fool.
Great men do make themselves, and are not made
By other men, or nature's accidents.
Themselves and God—the proudest can be humble
In rendering thanks to God. This is philosophy.
But here's Jahan. If he were not a king,
He might be a philosopher. That's something
To think of whiles I'm dumb.

[*Enter* SHAH JAHAN, *with* JAFAR KHAN *and* JAHANARA. JAHAN *wears his crown and is in the full dress of the emperor*.]

JAHAN: I am emperor still, and as an emperor
I will receive. The most courteous Aurungzeb,
Having destroyed my army, ta'en my city,
Relieved me of my many faithful friends—
Save such as have forgot to be unfaithful,
You, Jafar, and my daughter—
Guarded my palace in his care of me,
Craves audience. That's a subject's phrase:
Craves audience. There's no violence nor treason
In a petition that's so humbly couched,
And I,
The powerful and glorious Shah Jahan,
Do graciously permit. Where is my court?

JAFAR: Alas, your majesty,
Wound not yourself with fantasies that bite
More deeply than the fact.

JAHAN: Nay, but it is not a fantasy.
My court is there—Bahlol!
He was my eunuch yesterday. To-day
He is my soldiers, people, lords and ladies,
My office-bearers, writers, household servants,
And he shall kneel to me and kiss my hands.
Approach, Bahlol.

[BAHLOL *kneels to* JAHAN.]

Behold,
The homage of the world to Shah Jahan !

[*Distant shouting.*]

We'll mount our seat. Press not, my subjects—
My loving subjects—so closely on me.
We would have air.

JAHANARA : You are not
Your healthful self, good sir.
This audience put off. You Jafar——

JAHAN : What,'
We have some putting off to do, my girl,
That makes yours slight. Never
Has man put off so much as we shall do.

[*He mounts the throne. Shouting nearer.*]

Again that shouting. Aurungzeb
Plays well his instrument.
We are ready.

[*Enter* OFFICER.]

OFFICER : Prince Aurungzeb
Presents himself to th' Most Exalted Majesty,
The king valiant, Shah Jahan.

[*Enter* AURUNGZEB, MIR JUMLA, THE MULLAH, OFFICERS, *etc.* AURUNGZEB *kneels at the foot of the throne.*]

JAHAN : Rise, Aurungzeb. When last you left us,
You were a beggar—bereft of honour,
Of filial duty, and of soldiership.
Of our great clemency we pardoned you,
And bade you to redeem your squandered graces
As viceroy of the Deccan. You have done it.
We are well pleased and welcome your return.
Mir Jumla too—nay, of your modesty
Be not the servant.

[*He signs to* MIR JUMLA, *who kneels at the throne.*]

Rise, Mir Jumla,

We have expected you. When your late master,
Abdullah Shah, the king of Hyderabad,
Showed him ungrateful of your services,
And marched against you, you and your arms,
Your fealty, and the sworn adherence
Of head and heart you did transfer to us.
In recognition whereof
We have appointed you our minister.
You, Aurungzeb, shall be our chief commander.

[*He beckons* BAHLOL *to come forward.*]

There is your army, most ambitious sir—
Bahlol!
Mir Jumla,
Th' officials of the palace are before you—
Bahlol!
Gentlemen all,
You see our state. We are a happy king,
In having such a son and such a minister.
The Most Exalted Majesty of Hindostan,
The mighty Shah Jahan,
Greets each and all of you.

AURUNGZEB: Sir,
This mockery cannot serve.

JAHAN: Its name is Aurungzeb.

AURUNGZEB: What mean you?

JAHAN: Yours is the mockery—and you cannot serve.

AURUNGZEB: Not the same master. Hear me, majesty.

JAHAN: Majesty, Jafar. Jahanara,
You have a spendthrift brother. From his wealth
Of charméd words he flings me majesty,
Who else were naked.

AURUNGZEB: Your state, your person
Shall be protected. For your rule,
It is not for the good of Hindostan,
Nor for your own, that you should wear the crown.

I will not
Arraign you with th' abuses that have darkened
Your plenitude of power. Your subjects
Have suffered them, and what they have borne
Is my just title to the course I take.

JAHAN : O Mumtaz, Mumtaz,
When this—this smooth-lipped thief was in my hand,
And I had closed it on him, thou
Persuaded'st me to be gentle. Jahanara,
Thy voice was tuned to hers—see now,
What I am glad thy mother cannot see,
That kings who lack the colour to be cruel
Are by their children blasted. Sir, have done.
You are a subtle actor, but your play
Wearies my admiration. I'll to bed,
And sleep my night away, but ere I go
Of all the heavy garments of the day
I will divest myself. There is my crown.
Let him pick up who will.
Each several jewel in its glittering round
Is as a lightning that will pierce the wearer,
And burn and torture him. Now in a single step

[*Descending from the throne*]

I fall from glory to the common earth.
Great sir,
A private man—for not a dignity
Will I retain—you, who look on me here,
Know me no more, Jahan
Is now a shadow figure in a story—
A private man craves of your mastership
Leave to dwell i' the gardens of the Taj,
Aloof from the vain world. There with my daughter,
And the dead heart of me, will I wear out
What's left of nights and days. Your leave, great sir.

AURUNGZEB : You shall be cared for.

JAHAN : You palter with me. Cannot
Your crookedness unkink a single coil
And be one instant level. Answer then.
I' the gardens of the Taj I would retire.
Have I your leave ?

AURUNGZEB : Trouble not yourself with that.
We do not act from malice, nor forget
We are your son, nor will we wean
Our sister from you.

JAHAN : Equivocator. But we'll test
If loyalty has dregs in any breasts
That formerly owed service. Jahanara,
Attend your father. Gentlemen,
Make way for us. We go
Forever from this place.

[He attempts to leave by the outer entrance. At a sign from AURUNGZEB, MIR JUMLA *and the officers, etc. draw their swords and bar his exit.]*

His care of me. He will not
Suffer his father face the shelterless world,
And swords him from his freedom.
Here is indeed a son. Jahanara,
Attend thy father yet. Oh, oh,
I am nightmared by devils. See, ah see,
They grin at me, and yonder
Is the chief monster. What a sooty glare
He turns upon me. In, in, in.
I am beset. My guards. Ho !
My queen. They've murdered her.
Ah, see, see, see
The murderers with their swords.
It is a jest—a jest !

[He breaks into hysterical laughter, and is attended off by JAHANARA *and* JAFAR KHAN.*]*

MIR JUMLA (*taking up the crown and offering it on his knees to* AURUNGZEB) : Emperor of Hindostan !

[AURUNGZEB *holding the crown in his hands ascends the throne.*]

AURUNGZEB (*putting on the crown*) : There is no God but God !

[*All fall on their faces, and the scene closes.*]

END OF ACT IV.

ACT V

Scene I

AGRA. *A small chamber in the palace. A couch on the right, on which lies* JAHAN, *now aged and broken. A small window on the left.*

JAHAN, JAHANARA, *afterwards* OFFICER, AURUNGZEB.

JAHANARA : Are you awake, my father ?
JAHAN : I am dead,
And the dead wake not.
JAHANARA : Nay, my father,
You cannot so beiieve. The dead are free.
JAHAN : Beyond the grave perhaps, but I lie in it.
JAHANARA : Dear father, you are dreaming still.
An ill, ill dream. Awake, dear one. This is
Your chamber, and the humble Jahanara
Kneels at your couch, who are her happiness.
Will you not smile at her ?
JAHAN : This is my grave.
When I did live I sat upon a throne,
And stretched my hand, and took the world for mine.
Power crooked himself before me. Splendour
Apparelled me. Now I am kneaded
Into a clod, and rot—rot—rot.
What are you doing in this charnel house ?
Are you not quick ?
JAHANARA : Do you not know me then ?
My poor, poor father. You are wandering.
You must have a physician. Aurungzeb

G

Shall send you a physician. He will not
Deny us that.

JAHAN: Curses on Aurungzeb!
May the maleficent essence of all curses
That have been laid on all unnatural sons
From the beginning, concentrate on him!
And—and——

JAHANARA: Good sir, be calm. Nay, nay,
I will attend you—there, there, you shall feel
Better reclining so. The sunset hour
Is gracious.

JAHAN: How long have I been here?
Is't days, or months, or years?

JAHANARA: I count them not, my father. You and I
Are in so small a world, but all our own,
That time is little too.

JAHAN: How long? How long? Answer me. Is it years?

JAHANARA: Ten years, my father.

JAHAN: Ten—ten long, long weary years.
And I, whose scope
Was liberal as the wind's, no bounds
Of time or place, save such as my own will
Did give them circumscription, here immured,
Like one of my own beasts, whose to and fro
Scarce stretches his own length.
And you, whose wasted youth
Looks wanly from those cheeks, why do you stay
On an old, helpless man, the scorn and mock,
As well I know I must be, of those eyes
Which read their fate in mine—and now in *his*.
Have you no answer ready?

JAHANARA: I have a good one—I'm your daughter, sir.

JAHAN: My daughter, that's to say
That I begot you. Ha! ha! ha!
A most excelling and most puissant reason,
For what—for treachery, dethronement, murder,

For prison, torture, all the deeds of hell.
Men—ordinary men—beget
Things human like themselves, but kings
Breed only serpents, so the long line
Of the imperial reptiles fang each other,
And trail themselves in blood. What fool was I,
That I cursed Aurungzeb.
He is accursed as I in being royal.
We are bloody monsters all, and you,
In that you are my daughter, must be vile.
Ten years—and yet you have not poisoned me.
You serve Aurungzeb—nay, nay, why do you weep?

JAHANARA : My father, oh my father, I must weep,
Or else my heart will crack.
I prithee, sir, be patient with me. I
Lack words for what I feel.

JAHAN : Forgive me, Jahanara, daughter, saint,
Who art thy mother even in thy tears,
Which do rebuke me to her. Nay, nay, nay,
'Twas Shah Jahan who spoke so cruelly,
And he has vanished like a golden smoke.
Here's but a poor, decrepit, dying wretch, whose dregs
An angel tenders, till they vanish too.
Nor king, nor princess we, only
A father and his child.

JAHANARA : His loving child.

JAHAN : Her loving father, who must wonder yet
That thou art what thou art.

JAHANARA : Will you look forth,
As is your wont, before the night comes down.

JAHAN : This is the crown
Of each and all my days.
For this one moment every moment pays,
And still is huge in debt.
For this one moment am I still a king,
Grieving for such a queen.

Help me to the window.

[He looks out on the distant Taj.]

Is it a thing substantial, or a vision
That now I look on. Domes like bubbles,
On arches builded of immarbled air.
So delicate, yet with form. 'Tis even
As a lovely thought, floating in the mind's eye,
Ere that creation has ta'en hold of it,
And marred it in the taking. It meseems
The pleasure house of a bright and living spirit,
Towards which the musical waters lead
Even from this very window.
A pathway mirroring Heaven. I will tread it.
Mumtaz——

JAHANARA: Father.

JAHAN: The cypresses are black. It is a tomb.
Cold, cold and grey.
How could I think it other.

JAHANARA: The moon is early and sets with the sun.

JAHAN: My moon has set before me,
Going down in blood. I'll look no more.
Would I could think no more. This thinking
Sears me as with a knife.

JAHANARA: Would I could tender to you quietness,
And you would take it from me.

JAHAN: Quietness!
There is no quietness for kings. They live
In a prolonged delirium,
Drunken with thought or action matters not.
They are the chainéd followers of tempest,
And when they are blasted by it,
And being a king unkinged, are less than nothing,
They maw on memory.
Oh, it were better never to have been,
Than to have been and be.

JAHANARA : The foolish Jahanara begs you, sir,
To be in spirit, putting off the world
Which has so put off you.

JAHAN : It is not
As if I had been a commonplace of kings,
A gilded cut-throat, and a servile drab
Of brainless power. No, no, no.
Power was my handmaiden, the which I used
To create beauty, building
Temples and palaces, and out
Even of my desperate loss and kingly sorrow
Did carve the all-glorious Taj.
Fool, fool, now all my palaces be shrunk
Into this narrow prison. He who made
Acres of skyey splendour, eats his years
In this small *here*, where scarce might hang
The garments that he wore. A scullion's closet
Might yield superfluous space to cut it out,
Yet it is large enough to hold my fortunes,
Which are as skimped as it.
A couch, no more, to die on
Is the extent and utmost of my need.
And yet I'd not die so—but that's a thought
That must have utterance soon.
Is't not the wonted hour when my good son
Looks kindly on his ruin ?

JAHANARA : It is his hour.

JAHAN : And Agra holds its sovereign—say it does,
Or must I stay my going, if I can.

JAHANARA : Aurungzeb
Is from his hunting, sir. I heard
The trumpets blare his welcome whiles you slept.

JAHAN : And He hunts well. Tigers and kings
His trophies are.

[*Enter an* OFFICER.]

OFFICER : The emperor
Hopes that your health is better, and that you'll
Permit him pay his customary visit.
JAHAN : Tell the emperor
I am not but I shall be better, and
Impatience hold in leash till he is come.
OFFICER : It shall be carried to him.
[*Exit* OFFICER.]
JAHAN : He is
Of courteous guile, punctilious treachery,
The absolute master.
JAHANARA : Speak him, I pray you, fair, that he may send
Physician to you straight, for much I fear
That you are very ill.
JAHAN : Is not ten years enough ? Wouldst have me be
His set-off longer, let his triumph gloat
Over the spectacle of my misery ?
So fond a sister to her Aurungzeb,
That she would have her father live to tinct
With freshlier colour his ascendancy.
JAHANARA : Alas, alas.
Think not of the unhappy Jahanara,
Suspect as daughter, as a sister scorned.
Let her be nothing but a servitor,
To do commands and wait on you,
No more.
JAHAN : Nay, now you make me weep,
That love can be so bitter.
JAHANARA : No, no, no.
Love's bitterness is sweet, that it does give
Scope for love's bounty.
JAHAN : Yours, my Jahanara,
Is as your mother's, limitless.
So, so—we are at one again.
For a physician we'll not trouble Aurungzeb.
I have one at my hand, a skilful one,

Whose cure is certain.
Look not so strange, my maid.
As a vessel
Draining its waters gurgles at the last,
So do I seem to hear the bubbling ebb
Of my heart's drops.
The magnificent Shah Jahan,
The Ganges of whose glory spread so wide,
Shrinks to a trickle. Aurungzeb——

[*Enter* OFFICER.]

OFFICER : The emperor.

[*Enter* AURUNGZEB. *The* OFFICER *retires*.]

AURUNGZEB : Aurungzeb
To his august and honourable sire
Brings his respect and duty.

JAHAN : Does he indeed.
(*To* JAHANARA) My child,
If you'd observe humility with a tiara
Of principalities and kingdoms on his brow,
Look at your brother.

AURUNGZEB : The old man wanders, Jahanara.
How long has he been thus ?

JAHAN : He asks how long—*he* asks.
Tell him, ten years,
Ten years of prison, loneliness, and grief,
Wherein each cankering moment feels some little
Fragment of soul rot off, till there is left
The broken thing to which
He tenders his respect. Respect !
May hell confound you, boy.
Oh, oh, I choke.

JAHANARA : Quick, quick, my brother, a physician quick,
Or while we watch he passes.

AURUNGZEB : Physician shall be sent him instantly.

JAHAN : I will not have physician.
Stay the supremest mockery of all,

And let me finish mildly. I have yet
Something to speak.

AURUNGZEB: Even in this I shall obey you, sir.

JAHAN: And in what else obey?

AURUNGZEB: In aught
That it becomes you ask, and me to grant.

JAHAN: 'Tis a discreet obedience, and I'll not
Too much o'ertax it.
Grant then that in that hour
When son or kindred, or if you
Have with a better wisdom than I showed,
Cut them off timely, some as treacherous friend
Hurls you from splendour, blasts your state and function,
And holding death off as too sweet an end,
Condemns to cagéd madness, you will not
Forget Jahan. In that most certain hour
I would be in your thoughts. Will you do that?

AURUNGZEB: You shall be in my thought, as you have been,
And something of your wisdom have I already
Essayed. Dara and Murad—
I spared your tenderness in keeping from you
Th' anticipation of your own good counsel—
Cannot be danger more.

JAHAN: Did I not know't, though to my prison ears
All news is barred—but that they must be dead
Is implicate in this—that you are king.
And Shuja too?

AURUNGZEB: He wanders, where I know not.
So that you see, my father, I am safe,
As far as being brotherless can make me.

JAHAN: Admirable Aurungzeb.
By that how much thou hast out-crimsoned me,
Thou hast out-kinged me too.
I hated blood. It sickened me,
That monarchs may not monarchise who stint
The gory measure.

AURUNGZEB : Have you no commands
Further to lay upon me ?
JAHAN : My commands
Must not be proud as your humility,
But crook the knee and beg.
Give me your leave to die.
AURUNGZEB : To every man
Cometh his hour.
May yours,
If it be God's will, still be far off.
JAHAN : Most politic and most pious.
This God then it appears has human instruments,
Who on the gong of murder strike his doom,
And so do sound his will.
That, since you've graciously forborne his office
In my particular, is not in your scope.
A place to die in, is. Grant me but that,
And I'll wipe off some spots from the black scroll
Whereon your deeds are writ.
AURUNGZEB : My deeds let be. Your own
Claim all your scrutiny. Let it rest there,
For I must leave you.
JAHAN : A word. A word. This is the last
Of Shah Jahan. To-morrow
He'll trouble you no further.
Let me go off, even where I lived,
I' the presence of my wife. My tomb the Taj.
AURUNGZEB : You shall be buried there.
JAHAN : I pray you let me die there,
Sliding into the dark in the dim glory
Where all I ever loved, or who loved me—
Save Jahanara—dwells in the pomp
And circumstance of death.
Let me not pass hence like a cagéd beast,
But like a king who was, and when he was,
Loaded the earth with splendour.

Shed this one ray of greatness o'er the ruin
On which you stand enthroned.
I do but beg a grave, for I shall never
Pass out again.

JAHANARA : Listen, my brother, and be pitiful.
If aught that Jahanara says can move you,
Let this request be granted, and when she's
Immured with God, she'll pray for you.
Ah, Aurungzeb,
How many else will offer prayers for you,
That you can dare despise poor Jahanara's.

AURUNGZEB : My sister, if I could
Subdue my spirit, it would be to yours—but this,
This is an old man's fantasy,
A trick of age—and yet
I'll be a fool to folly. Sir, you shall
Be this night secretly transported
To the Taj. If ere the dawn
Your spark be quenched not, it shall be put out.
And so I serve your pleasure.
Now farewell.

JAHAN : Farewell and thanks,
Thanks and farewell. This, Aurungzeb,
Cancels the heavy years.

[*Exit* AURUNGZEB. JAHAN *goes to the window.*]

Thou horrid chamber,
You portal me to *that* (*pointing to the Taj*).

JAHANARA : Gently, good sir, lest you
Forestal your leave-taking and I
Am cheated of my little time to serve you.
It has been sweet to daughter you, my father.
Soon we'll say
Good-night to one another.

JAHAN : What have I done
To deserve you, Jahanara.

[*The scene closes.*]

SCENE 2

AGRA. *The interior of the Taj Mahal. A single torch illumines the darkness, permitting little to be seen beyond the white gleam of the cenotaph.*

JAHAN, *afterwards the* GHOST OF MUMTAZ.

JAHAN : Thou flickering flame,
Thou hastenest to the dark. May I
Precede you there. The day
Is long behind me, and a slow setting
Ends where my light began, the dawn and noon
Of all that made me royal,
Casketed richly in this wonder-house,
Wherein my grief's immortal.
Here have I writ my story.
Jahan, who loved and lost.
All else
Is but a beggar's tale—this is a king's.
His state, his triumphs, subjects, empery,
Rayed to one centre, took their colour
From that one flawless glass,
The heart of Mumtaz.
Mumtaz. Mumtaz. Is there no spell,
No magic in that name,
To stir the utter silence of this place,
Which now appals me.
Nothing. Nothing. Tombs do but mock us,
And horribly perpetuate the cheats
That happiness with grinning craft prepares
To damn us at its leaving.
You fretted roof,
Fall on me, crush me. Let my handiwork
Be dust with me. Mumtaz was murdered.
Why do you then hold off ?

[*The* Ghost of Mumtaz *appears*.]

Some madness clouds my brain,
Or is't the mausoleum's delicate tracery
That my sick fancy, ere it faints away,
Shapes to the semblance and the guise of her.
Would I might die now, while it looks at me
With such a fixéd tenderness. If this
Is self-created, 'tis a mockery
That betters substance.
I dare not speak to it,
Lest, being an apparition born of silence,
A sound should banish it. So like——

Ghost : Jahan.

Jahan : Is it of me, or of itself,
A visitant from some dim realm of afterwards,
Or only
Disguiséd death, to mark
My hour is done.

Ghost : Jahan.

Jahan : The wreck and waste of him,
Now passing
Into his long oblivion.
If you be his love,
And not an exhalation from the embers
Of his expiring spirit, speak again
That name of misery.

Ghost : Jahan.

Jahan : Mumtaz. I will no longer doubt.
It is my love—the love of Shah Jahan,
Walking the earth, and yet not of it.
Whence are you, that you steal
Into my sight, that awe and wonder
Confound my natural man ?

Ghost : Perchance
I am thyself, Jahan, who in this hour
Of dissolution,

Does on the mortal script which is thy body,
Write his most brief comment.

JAHAN : I'll not believe it.
But whatso'er thou art, spirit or thought,
Thou comest in so exquisite a semblance,
Thou canst not speak me wrong . . .
Thou art silent.
Hear then Jahan
Sum up his history :
Jahan, who was the slave
Of two contending passions,
His love of beauty, and his love of thee.
They were his inspiration, and his fall.
His fall, Mumtaz, and yet
While he has breathing, they have breathing too,
But falter not with his. Oh, speak again,
Nor look at me so strangely.

GHOST : Shah Jahan, O Shah Jahan,
Thou lovedst thyself, and thy magnificence.
These other loves were but as garments
To clothe thy splendours, mightily setting off
Their poorer betters.
Thy love of beauty was a lust,
Wherein compassion, sacrifice and pity,
Found in't no glass to show them.
Thy love for me, though in the innermost
True to itself, was in the shell and gloss of it
A trick and glitter on thy majesty,
Debasing its own heraldry in thine.
From this thy web of juggle and delusion
Shake thyself free, and let thyself
See thyself as thou art, ere seer and seen
Alike dislimn. Thou hast
No more to do,
Nor this, that shapéd out of shadows,
Returns to them again.

JAHAN : Stay, thou dread apparition.
Thou strip'st me to the quick,
Barin'g my naked soul to the raw sight,
That filmless, damns its former flattery.
Art thou indeed Mumtaz ? Thy words
Speak'st thou in love or hate ?

GHOST : Jahan.

JAHAN : In love then. If thou lov'st
Thou liv'st. The Taj
Clips not the all of thee.
Say that thou liv'st,
And that in some bright otherwhere
I shall not miss thee.

GHOST : Jahan.

[*The phantom vanishes.*]

JAHAN : It's gone.
Gone on that word " Jahan."
Let me—O powers
Whate'er ye are, that wait
On mortal passing—let the pendulum
Of my spent spirit stop,
Now, even now, as I
Utter that name, wherein what's best
Of this poor shred and remnant of a man
Inheres and turns—
Mumtaz . . .

[*The torch goes out.*]

END OF THE PLAY.